Nick Vandome

Windows 8

in
easy steps

In easy steps is an imprint of In Easy Steps Limited
4 Chapel Court · 42 Holly Walk · Leamington Spa
Warwickshire · United Kingdom · CV32 4YS
www.ineasysteps.com

Notice of Liability
Every effort has been made to ensure that this book contains accurate
and current information. However, In Easy Steps Limited and the
author shall not be liable for any loss or damage suffered by readers
as a result of any information contained herein.

Trademarks
Microsoft® and Windows® are registered trademarks of Microsoft
Corporation. All other trademarks are acknowledged as belonging to
their respective companies.

In Easy Steps Limited supports The Forest Stewardship Council (FSC),
the leading international forest certification organisation. All our titles
that are printed on Greenpeace approved FSC certified paper carry the
FSC logo.

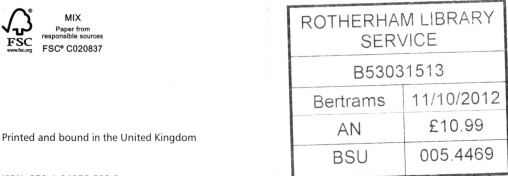

FSC
www.fsc.org

MIX
Paper from
responsible sources
FSC® C020837

Printed and bound in the United Kingdom

ISBN 978-1-84078-538-8

Contents

11 Networking 205

12 System and Security 219

Index 233

1 Introducing Windows 8

This chapter explains what Windows is and what is new in Windows 8; including the new Windows 8 interface, Charms and touch screen capabilities.

What is Windows?

Windows is an operating system for PCs (personal computers). The operating system is the software that organizes and controls all of the components (hardware and software) in your computer so that they integrate and work efficiently together.

The first operating system from Microsoft was known as MS-DOS (Microsoft Disk Operating System). This was a non-graphical, line-oriented, command-driven operating system, able to run only one application at a time.

The original Windows system was an interface manager that ran on top of the MS-DOS system, providing a graphical user interface and using clever processor and memory management to allow it to run more than one application or function at a time.

The basic element of Windows was its "windowing" capability. A window (with a lower-case w) is a rectangular area used to display information or to run a program. Several windows can be opened at the same time so that you can work with multiple applications. This provided a dramatic increase in productivity when using PCs, in comparison with the original MS-DOS.

Microsoft released four versions of this interface management Windows, with numerous intermediate versions, including:

- 1985 – Windows 1.0

- 1987 – Windows 2.0, 2.1 and 2.11

- 1990 – Windows 3.0, 3.1, 3.11 (Windows for Workgroups)

- 1995 – Windows 95, 98, 98 SE and Me (Millennium Edition)

The next version, Windows XP, was a full operating system in its own right. This was eventually followed by Windows Vista:

- 2001 – Windows XP (eXPerience) Home and Professional

- 2007 – Windows Vista Home, Home Premium, Ultimate etc

- 2009 – Windows 7 Starter, Home Premium, Ultimate etc

About Windows 8

The latest version of Windows was released in 2012.

- 2012 – Windows 8, Windows 8 Pro and Windows RT. This is the eighth major version (as Microsoft views the Windows product release cycle)

One of the main developments with Windows 8 is that it is designed to work equally well on touch screen devices and traditional computers. The number of versions of Windows 8 has been consolidated too, compared with previous versions and there are now three main options on offer.

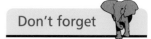

The Windows logo has also been redesigned, to make it look more like a window and less like a flag, as in previous versions.

Windows 8

This is the main consumer version of the software. It is a fully-featured version including all of the new features such as the new Windows 8 interface, Windows 8 apps, the improved File Explorer and Internet Explorer 10 which has versions for both the Windows 8 interface and the traditional Desktop environment. Windows 8 is designed to work equally effectively on desktop PCs, laptops and also touch screen computers and tablets. This version of Windows 8 can be upgraded to from, among others, Windows 7 Starter, Home Basic and Home Premium.

Windows 8 Pro

This is targeted more towards the business user. It contains all of the features in the Windows 8 version plus added features for security encryption and PC management. If you are upgrading from Windows 7 Professional or Ultimate then this is the version to use.

Windows RT

This version of Windows 8 is only available pre-installed on PCs and tablets with ARM processors, which help with a lightweight design and improved battery life for mobile devices. The RT version also comes with a pre-installed version of Microsoft Office (Word, Excel, Powerpoint and OneNote) that is optimized for use on touch screen devices.

Windows 8 Interface

Windows 8 is the most significant change to the Windows operating system since Windows 95 helped redefine the way that we look at personal computers. The most obvious change in Windows 8 is the new Windows 8 interface. This will be the first view of Windows 8 and all of the elements are accessed through the brightly colored Start screen.

The Windows 8 interface defines one of the main purposes of Windows 8: it is an operating system designed for the mobile generation so it will work in the same way on a desktop, laptop or tablet computer. It is the same operating system for all of these devices and it is also possible to synchronize Windows 8 so that all of your settings and apps will be available over multiple devices through an online Microsoft Account.

Another innovation in Windows 8 is the greater use of custom apps (applications) that are accessed from the Start screen. This is done through the colored tiles: each tile gives access to the relevant app. For instance, if you click or tap on the Photos app you will be able to view, organize and edit your photo files and folders. A lot of the Windows 8 apps are linked together too, so it is easy to share content through your apps. There are also a number of Windows 8 Charms that can be accessed at any point within Windows 8 to give a range of functionality. These can be accessed from the right-hand side of the screen.

Windows 8 is also optimized for touch screen use, so it is ideal for using with a tablet (such as the Microsoft Surface) where all of the screen navigation can be done by tapping, swiping and pinching on the screen. These features can also be used on desktops and laptops that have this functionality.

Even though Windows 8 has a very modern look with the Windows 8 interface, the old favorites such as the Desktop are not far away. The Desktop and all of its functionality that users have got used to with previous versions of Windows is available at the click or tap of a button and this takes you into an environment that, initially, may be more familiar.

Don't forget

Most leading laptop manufactuers now have a range of touch screen laptops, such as the Acer Aspire S7 and S5, HP's Envy TouchSmart and Spectre and Sony's VAIO T and VAIO E. There are also various tablets and hybrids, which are tablets with docking and keyboard facilities.

Beware

It can take a little time getting used to working with the two interfaces.

In a way, Windows 8 can be thought of as two operating systems that have been merged: the new Windows 8 interface, with its reliance on apps; and the traditional Windows interface with access to items through the Desktop.

Navigating Windows 8

Since Windows 8 is optimized for use with touch screen devices this introduces a new factor when it comes to navigating around the system, particularly the new Windows 8 interface. The three ways of doing this are:

- Mouse
- Keyboard
- Touch

Some of these methods can be used in conjunction with each other (for instance mouse and keyboard, and touch and keyboard) but the main ways of getting around Windows 8 with each are:

Mouse

- Move the mouse to the bottom left-hand corner to access the Start screen. Click on it once when it appears. this can be done from any app or the Desktop

Don't forget

One of the most obvious changes on the Start screen is how to turn off or restart your Windows 8 computer (see page 58).

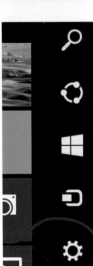

- Move the cursor over the top or bottom right-hand corners to access the Charms bar. Move down and click on one to access it

- Move the cursor over the top left-hand corner to view the most recently-used app. Click on it to access it

- Move the cursor over the top left-hand corner and drag down the left-hand side to view all of the currently-open apps (App Switcher). Click on one to access it

- In an open Windows 8 app, right-click to access the bottom toolbar. This will have options specific to the app in use

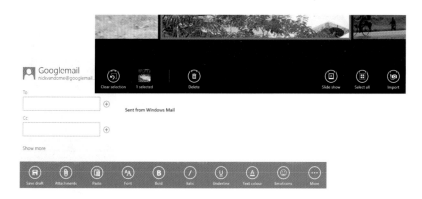

Don't forget

You can also close a Windows 8 app with the mouse by accessing the App Switcher and right-clicking on one of the apps and then clicking on the **Close** button.

- In an open Windows 8 app, click and hold at the top of the window and drag down to the bottom of the screen to close the app

...cont'd

Keyboard

The majority of the keyboard shortcuts for navigating around Windows 8 are accessed in conjunction with the WinKey. Press:

- **WinKey** to access the Start screen at any time

- **WinKey** + **L** to lock the computer and display the Lock screen

- **WinKey** + **C** to access the Charms bar

- **WinKey** + **I** to access the Settings Charm

- **WinKey** + **K** to access the Devices Charm

- **WinKey** + **H** to access the Sharing Charm

- **WinKey** + **Q** to access the Search Charm to search over apps

- **WinKey** + **F** to access the Search Charm to search over files

- **WinKey** + **D** to access the Desktop

- **WinKey** + **M** to access the Desktop with the active window minimized

- **WinKey** + **E** to access File Explorer, displaying the Computer folder

- **WinKey** + **T** to display the thumbnails on the Desktop Taskbar

- **WinKey** + **U** to access the Ease of Access Center

- **WinKey** + **X** to access administration tools and quick access to items including the Desktop and the Control Panel

- **WinKey** + **Z** in a Windows 8 app to display the app's toolbar at the bottom of the screen

- **Alt** + **F4** to close a Windows 8 app

- **Ctrl** + **Shift** + **Esc** to access the Task Manager

Touch

To navigate around Windows 8 with a touch screen device:

- Tap on an item to access it

- Swipe inwards from the right-hand edge to access the Charms bar

- Swipe inwards from the left-hand edge to switch between currently-open apps

- Swipe inwards slowly from the left-hand edge and drag one of the apps away from the App Switcher to snap it to the left-hand side

- Swipe inwards from the left and then back again to show the currently-open apps (App Switcher)

- In an open Windows 8 app, swipe upwards from the bottom of the screen, or downwards from the top of the screen, to access the app's toolbar

- In an open Windows 8 app, swipe down from inside the app to view its settings

- In an open Windows 8 app, hold at the top of the screen and drag down to the bottom to close the app

- On the Start screen, swipe down on an app's tile to view additional options relating to the app

- Pinch outwards to minimize the Start screen. Pinch inwards to return to normal view

15

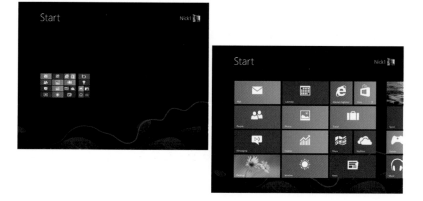

PC Requirements

The recommended specifications for PCs running Windows 8 are based on the processor mode used. On most current processors, you have the choice of 32-bit or 64-bit mode.

Windows 8 for 32-bit Processor Mode
The PC should have these minimum hardware requirements:

- Processor   1 GHz
- System Memory   1 GB
- Graphics   SVGA (800x600)
- Graphics adapter   DirectX9 class with WDDM 1.0 driver
- Graphics memory   128 MB (for Aero support)
- Hard Disk   16 GB available space
- Other   DVD-RW optical drive

Windows 8 for 64-bit Processor Mode
The PC should have these minimum hardware requirements:

- Processor   1 GHz
- System Memory   2 GB
- Graphics   SVGA (800x600)
- Graphics adapter   DirectX9 class with WDDM 1.0 driver
- Graphics memory   128 MB (for Aero support)
- Hard Disk   20 GB
- Other   DVD-RW optical drive

Windows Virtual PC requires a PC with Intel-VT or AMD-V enabled in the CPU, since the software relies on hardware virtualization features.

If you want to upgrade your existing PC to run Windows 8, you can run the Windows 8 Upgrade Assistant (see page 18) to identify any potential problems or short-comings.

32-Bit versus 64-Bit

As well as choosing your Windows 8 edition, you also need to decide between the 32-bit and the 64-bit versions of the operating system. This choice is available for all editions of Windows 8 with the retail packs including installation DVDs for each modes.

The 32-bit or 64-bit nomenclature refers to the memory address length which the processor can reference. This dictates the maximum amount of memory, which is 4 GB for 32-bit mode (or more exactly 3.4 GB, since some memory needs to be allocated to other purposes). For 64-bit mode, the maximum may be much higher, though the Windows 8 editions do not make full use of the potential. As well as more memory, 64-bit mode will also be faster, typically about 10%.

However, you need applications that are specifically optimized for 64-bit processing to take advantage of the speed improvements and memory increase. Many games for example include the necessary enhancements.

Remember that choosing a 64-bit system means that you can no longer run 16-bit applications. This is only a problem if you use very old software (from the Windows 3.1 days).

More seriously, existing 32-bit drivers for your devices will not operate in 64-bit mode, so you will have to locate 64-bit versions of the drivers. You may have problems with some devices, particularly the older ones.

You may also find that running 32-bit applications in a 64-bit operating system might actually be slower, due to the additional overheads imposed by conversion between the address systems.

In summary, if you have a 64-bit capable computer but use older hardware or 32-bit applications, you might do better to stay with the 32-bit version of Windows 8. With the latest hardware and drivers, and applications that are 64-bit optimized, for especially demanding applications such as video editing or image packages, the switch to 64-bit and higher memory would offer significant improvements.

It will not be long before 64-bit computing becomes the standard, and 32-bit operation becomes an optional extra, but for the present there are still large numbers of 32-bit applications.

Beware

If your computer is more than a few years old, it is quite possible that you can only run the 32-bit version of Windows 8.

17

Installing Windows 8

As with many things to do with Windows 8, the installation process has been simplified as much as possible. Depending on how you have obtained Windows 8 the options are:

- Upgrade – Replace an older version of Windows, retaining the installed applications and settings

- Dual Boot – Install Windows 8 while retaining the existing version of Windows, using a second disk partition. You'll need to install required applications to the new system

- Clean Install – Add Windows 8 to a newly-formatted disk, then install all required applications

- Pre-install – Buy a new PC with Windows 8 already installed, then install the required apps

When you have an existing version of Windows on your PC, you can purchase an Upgrade version of Windows 8, which will be at a reduced price from the full version.

In previous versions of Windows there was an Upgrade Advisor that checked your PC to see if there were any issues in regard to updating to the next version of Windows. However, with Windows 8 this is all incorporated into the Windows 8 Setup process itself. If you are upgrading from a previous version of Windows there is a Windows 8 Upgrade Assistant that will help with the installation process. Initially it will check the compatibility of your current setup and apps and flag up any issues. Then the installation will go through the following steps:

- Product key. This will be needed if you install your copy of Windows 8 from a DVD

- Personalize. These are settings that will be applied to your version of Windows 8. They include the color for the Start screen, a name for your computer and a connection to a wireless network. These settings can be selected within PC Settings once Windows 8 has been installed too

- Settings. You can choose to have express settings applied, or customize them

- Microsoft Account. You can set up a Microsoft Account during installation, or once you have started Windows 8

2 Getting Started

In many ways Windows 8 is one of the most radical new versions in the operating system's history. It places Windows very firmly in the mobile computing environment and many of its features are inspired by the Windows Phone interface. This chapter looks at some of the main changes, focusing on the new Start screen and the new interface. It shows how to navigate around these and organize them so that you can quickly feel comfortable using Windows 8.

Using a Microsoft Account

Don't forget

The Microsoft Account, and related services, replaces the Windows Live function. However, there will still be remnants of this online for some time and login details for this can be used for the Microsoft Account services.

Beware

Without a Windows Account you will not be able to access the apps listed here.

Hot tip

Microsoft Account details can also be used as your sign-in for Windows 8 (see page 21).

We live in a world of ever-increasing computer connectivity, where users expect to be able to access their content wherever they are and share it with their friends and family in a variety of ways, whether it is by email, messaging or photo sharing. This is known as cloud computing, with content being stored on online servers, from where it can be accessed by authorized users.

In Windows 8 this type of connectivity is achieved with a Microsoft Account. This is a registration system (which can be set up with most email addresses and a password) that provides access to a number of services via the Windows 8 apps. These include:

- Mail. This is the Windows 8 email app that can be used to access and manage your different email accounts

- Messaging. This is the text messaging app

- People. This is the address book app

- Calendar. This is the calendar and organizer app

- The Windows Store. This is the online store for previewing and downloading additional apps

- SkyDrive. This is the online sharing service

Creating a Microsoft Account

It is free to create a Microsoft Account and can be done with an online email address and, together with a password, this provides a unique identifier for logging into your Microsoft Account and the related apps. There are several ways in which you can create and set up a Microsoft Account:

- During the initial setup process when you install Windows 8. You will be asked if you want to create a Microsoft Account at this point. If you do not, you can always do so later

- When you first open an app that requires access to a Microsoft Account. When you do this you will be prompted to create a new account

- From the Users section of the PC settings that are accessed from the Settings Charm (for more information about the PC settings see pages 36–45)

Whichever way you use to create a Microsoft Account the process is similar:

1 When you are first prompted to Sign in with a Microsoft Account, click or tap on the **Sign up for a Microsoft account** link

2 Enter an email address and a password

3 Click or tap on the **Next** button to move through the registration process

Next

4 Enter additional information including your name, location and zip/post code. On the next screen you also need to enter a phone number, which is used as a security measure by Microsoft if you forget your password

5 Click or tap on the **Finish** button to complete setting up your Microsoft Account

Don't forget

If you create a Microsoft Account when accessing a related app, the sign-up process will take you to the online Account Live web page, but the process is similar. In both cases you will be able to login to the Account Live web page too, at https://login.live.com. You can also access your account details at https://account.live.com

21

Sign-in Options

Each time you start up your computer you will need to sign in. This is a security feature so that no-one else can gain unauthorized access to your account on your PC. This sign-in process starts with the Lock screen and then you have to enter your login password.

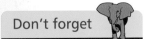
1 When you start your PC the Lock screen will be showing. This can only be opened by your password

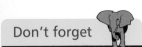
2 Click or tap on the **Lock screen**, or press any key, to move to the login screen. Enter your password and press **Enter** or click or tap on this arrow

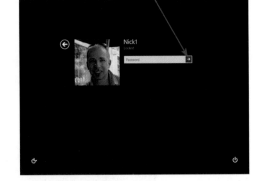

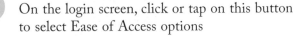
3 On the login screen, click or tap on this button to select Ease of Access options

4 Click or tap on this button to select Power off options including Shut Down and Restart

22

5 On the login screen, click or tap on this button to view the login screen for all users on the PC

Don't forget

You can sign in with a local account or a Microsoft Account. If you sign in with the latter you will have access to the related services, such as Mail, Messaging and People. Also, you will be able to sync your settings and use them from another computer if you login there with your Microsoft Account.

6 Click or tap on another user to access their own login screen

Login settings

Settings for how you login can be accessed from the Users section in the PC settings:

Don't forget

For details about accessing and using PC settings see pages 36–45.

1 Access the PC settings and click or tap on the **Users** button

2 Select options to change your password, create a picture password or create a PIN instead of a password

3 If you want to create a picture password you have to have a touch screen device. Select a picture and draw a pattern to use as your login

23

Adding Users

If more than one person uses the computer, each person can have a user account defined with a user name and a password. To create a new user account, as either a Microsoft Account, or as a local account.

1. Access the PC settings as shown on page 36 and click or tap on the **Users** button

2. Under Other users, click or tap on the **Add a user** button

Other users

+ Add a user

3. To add a user with a Microsoft Account, enter an email address

Add a user

What email address would this person like to use to sign in to Windows? (If you know the email address they use to sign in to Microsoft services, enter it here.)

Email address

When you sign in to Windows with a Microsoft account, you can:
- Download apps from Windows Store.
- Get your online content in Microsoft apps automatically.
- Sync settings online to make PCs look and feel the same–this includes settings like browser favorites and history.

Privacy statement

Sign up for a new email address

Sign in without a Microsoft account

Next   Cancel

4. Click or tap on the **Next** button (see Step 10)

5. To create a local account, click or tap on the **Sign in without a Microsoft account** link

Sign in without a Microsoft account

24

6　At this stage you will still be encouraged to login with a Microsoft Account and information about both types is displayed

7　Click or tap on the **Local account** button

8　Enter a user name, a password and a password hint in case the password is forgotten

9　Select this box if it is a child's account and you want it to be monitored by the Family Safety feature

10　For a Microsoft Account, more information is required. Enter the relevant details in the fields and select the **Next** button to complete the additional windows in the registration process

Hot tip

Family Safety settings can be applied in the Family Safety section in the Control Panel. It is accessed under the User Accounts and Family Safety section. Click or tap on a user and then settings can be applied for items such as web filtering, time controls and app restrictions.

The Start Screen

The first, and most obvious, difference about Windows 8 over previous versions of Windows, is that the Start Button is no more. This was the button in the bottom left-hand corner of the screen from which programs and various areas of the computer were accessed. In Windows 8 this has been replaced by the Start screen, which is part of the new Windows 8 interface.

The Start screen is a collection of large, brightly colored tiles. By default these are the apps (programs) which are provided with Windows 8. At first sight, the Start screen is a big change from previous Windows' interfaces. But don't panic: there is considerable functionality on the Start screen for finding items, getting around and customizing your Windows 8 experience. Also, it is still possible to access your old Windows favorites such as the Desktop and the Control Panel.

First view

Once you sign in from the Lock screen the Start screen is the first thing you will see:

Don't forget

It may take a little time to get used to the new Start screen compared to previous versions of Windows. However, the more you use it the more you will begin to exploit the potential of this ground-breaking version of Windows.

The Windows 8 apps are shown as colored tiles. These are the built-in apps that have been designed specifically for use with Windows 8. Much of the functionality of the Start screen works best with these apps.

Another change in Windows 8 is that there are no scroll bars visible on the Start screen. However, they are still there and can be used to view the rest of the apps on the Start screen:

1 Move the cursor over the bottom of the screen to access the scroll bar and scroll to the right to view all of the apps on the Start screen

When you are working in any app, the Start screen can be accessed at any time by moving the cursor over the bottom left-hand corner of the screen. When the Start screen icon appears, click or tap on it to move to the Start screen.

Beware

Move the cursor fully into the bottom left-hand corner to access the Start screen icon. Click or tap on the icon while the cursor still feels as if it has gone off the edge of the screen. If you move the cursor first then the Start screen icon may disappear.

Around the Start Screen

In addition to accessing the default apps on the Start screen, there is also a range of functionality that can be accessed by moving the cursor over the edges and corners of the screen:

1. Move the cursor over the bottom or top right-hand corners to access the Charms bar. These are five icons that can be used for a variety of functions (see pages 30–33 to see details about the Charms)

Don't forget

The Charms bar can also be accessed by swiping in from the right-hand side of the screen on a touch screen device, or using **WinKey** + **C** on a keyboard.

2. Click or tap on the bottom **Charm** (Settings) to access the relevant settings for the Start screen

Don't forget

For more information about the default Start screen Settings see pages 34–35.

28

3 Move the cursor over the top left-hand corner to view the most recently-accessed app. Click or tap on it to access it

4 Drag down from the top left-hand corner to view all of the currently-open apps. Click or tap on one to access it

Don't forget

One option in Step 4 is the Desktop which displays the most recently-used item on the Desktop, regardless of how many apps are open there.

Charms

As shown on the page 28, the Charms can be accessed by moving the cursor over the bottom or top right-hand corners of the screen. The Charms are, from top to bottom:

- Search

- Sharing

- Start screen

- Devices

- Settings

The Charms can be accessed at any time, from any app, by moving the cursor over the bottom or top right-hand corners of the screen. Therefore if you want to access, for instance, the Start screen while you are working in the Photos app this can be done with the Start screen Charm.

Settings

The Settings Charm can be used to access the Start screen Settings and also PC settings for personalizing the Start screen (see page 38 for more details). It can also be accessed from any app and used for settings for that specific app. So, if you are working in the Mail app and select the Settings Charm, you will be provided with the Mail Settings. Or, if you are in Internet Explorer you will be provided with settings for this and so on. To use the Settings Charm:

Don't forget

When you access the Charms bar, a separate panel displays the date, time, Wi-Fi connection and battery charge level (if using a laptop).

1 Access the Charms and click or tap on the **Settings Charm**

2 At the bottom of the panel are the default settings that are always available from the Settings Charm

3 At the top of the panel are settings specific to the Start screen

4 Open an app and select the **Settings Charm**. The default settings are still available at the bottom of the panel, but the top now has settings options for the active app, i.e. the one currently being used. For example, these are the settings for Internet Explorer 10

Devices

The Devices Charm can be used to send items in an app to any available device. For instance, if you are viewing a photo in the Photos app, you can use the Devices Charm to send it to any available printers. To use the Devices Charm:

1 Access the Charms and click or tap on the **Devices Charm**

2 Select a Device. The related task will then be undertaken, i.e. an item will be sent to a printer

Beware

The Devices Charm only works from compatible devices on the Start screen, but not the Desktop. For instance, the Photos app will usually have printer devices available, but if you open a word processing app, such as Word, on the Desktop then there will be no devices available from the Devices Charm. However, items such as printers can still be accessed from the app's Menu bar on the Desktop as in previous versions of Windows.

...cont'd

Start screen Charm

Click or tap on this Charm to return to the Start screen at any point from within Windows 8.

Sharing Charm

The Sharing Charm can be used to share items within an app with the suite of apps, including Mail and People (the address book app). To use the Sharing Charm

1. Access the Charms and click or tap on the **Sharing Charm**

2. Select the app with which you want to share the current content. This could involve emailing a photo to someone or sending a web page directly to a contact in the People app

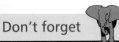

Don't forget

To use the Share Charm you have to first select an item in an appropriate app, i.e. select a photo in the Photos app, rather than just open the app.

Search Charm

The Search Charm can be used to search for items within the app in which you are working. For instance, if the Video app is open then the search will be conducted over this by default.

The Search Charm can also be used to search over your computer and your apps. To use the Search Charm

1 Access the Charms and click on the **Search Charm**

2 Select an area over which you want to perform the search, e.g. Settings in this case

3 When working in an app, select the **Search Charm**. This can automatically be used to search over the app which you are currently using

Charm Shortcuts

The individual Charms can also be accessed with keyboard shortcuts. These are:

- All Charms: **WinKey** + **C**
- Settings Charm: **WinKey** + **I**
- Devices Charm: **WinKey** + **K**
- Start screen: **WinKey**
- Sharing Charm: **WinKey** + **H**
- Search Charm: **WinKey** + **Q**

Default Settings

As shown on page 30 some of the settings on the Settings Charm are available whenever this is accessed, regardless of which app you are in. To use these:

1 Access the Settings Charm by moving the cursor over the bottom or top right-hand corners and click or tap on this icon

2 The default settings appear at the bottom of the panel, above the Change PC settings link

3 Click or tap on this button to access Network and Wi-Fi settings

Hot tip

You can connect to, and disconnect from, network connections in the Networks Setting, by selecting the name of a network and selecting either the Connect or Disconnect button.

4 If you have moved to a level down in the Settings structure, click or tap on this button at the top of the panel to move back to the previous level

5 Click or tap on this button to adjust the volume. Drag this slider to make the adjustment

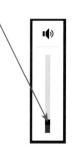

6 Click or tap on this button to adjust the screen brightness. Drag this slider to make the adjustment

Notifications can be set for a variety of apps so that you are alerted when there is new information. Settings for notifications can be selected within the Notifications section of the PC settings (see page 40).

7 Click or tap on this button to specify timescales for when notifications appear

Hide for 8 hours

Hide for 3 hours

Hide for 1 hour

8 Click or tap on this button to access options for shutting down and restarting the computer (see page 58 for more details)

9 If a virtual keyboard is available, click or tap on this button to access its settings

Unavailable

Personalize Settings

The Settings Charm enables you to set the appearance of the Lock screen, the Start screen and select an account photo. To do this first access the PC settings:

1 Access the Charms and click or tap on the **Settings Charm**

2 Click or tap on the **Change PC settings** link

Change PC settings

3 Click or tap on the **Personalize** button underneath the PC settings heading

PC settings

Personalize

Personalizing the Lock screen

To personalize the Lock screen:

1 Click or tap on the **Lock screen** link at the top of the Personalize page

PC settings ──────→ Lock screen

Personalize

2 Click or tap on one of the thumbnail images to select a new image for the Lock screen

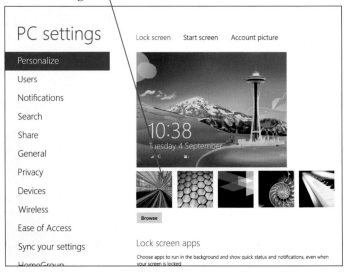

PC settings

Lock screen   Start screen   Account picture

Personalize
Users
Notifications
Search
Share
General
Privacy
Devices
Wireless
Ease of Access
Sync your settings
HomeGroup

10:38
Tuesday 4 September

Browse

Lock screen apps
Choose apps to run in the background and show quick status and notifications, even when your screen is locked

Beware

The Personalize PC settings only apply to the new interface elements of Windows 8, i.e. the Start screen, Lock screen and account photo. The Desktop can be personalized using the Control Panel as in previous versions of Windows. For more information about this see Chapter Five.

3 The selected image becomes the Lock screen background

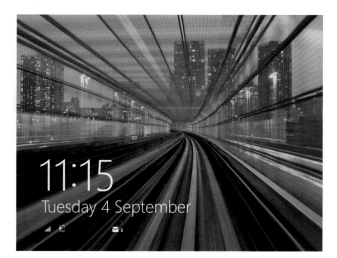

Don't forget

Notifications can be set to appear on the Lock screen. Do this under the Lock screen apps heading in the Personalize section of PC settings.

4 Click or tap on the **Browse** button to select an image from your hard drive for the Lock screen background

5 Select an image and click or tap on **Choose picture** to set the image as the Lock screen background

Hot tip

If you use your own images for the Lock screen background, these will remain available on the thumbnail row even if you switch to another image for the background.

6 The image is added as the background for the Lock screen

...cont'd

Personalizing the Start screen

There are also settings for the appearance of the Start screen:

1. Click or tap on the **Start screen** link at the top of the Personalize page

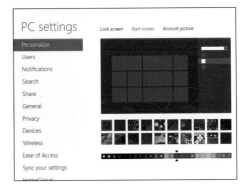

2. The settings enable you to change the background color and pattern

3. Click or tap on one of these thumbnails to select a background pattern

4. Drag this slider to select a background color

5. The selections in Steps 3 and 4 are applied to the Start screen background

Don't forget

The color scheme for the background, i.e. the different shades, are preset for each color and cannot be changed.

Personalizing the Account Photo

To set your own photo for your personal account:

1 Click or tap on the **Account picture** link at the top of the Personalize page

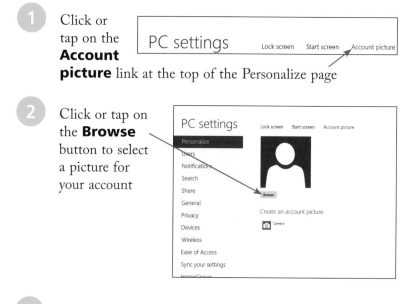

PC settings   Lock screen   Start screen   Account picture

2 Click or tap on the **Browse** button to select a picture for your account

3 Select a photo or picture and click or tap on the **Choose picture** button to add it as your account picture

4 The photo is displayed on the Personalize screen

5 The photo is also displayed at the top right-hand corner of the Start screen where you can lock the screen or change users

Nick

Users settings

Select the **Users** button to select options for switching accounts, changing your password and adding more users (see pages 24–25).

Don't forget

The Users settings can be used to switch between a Microsoft Account and a local account for signing in to your PC.

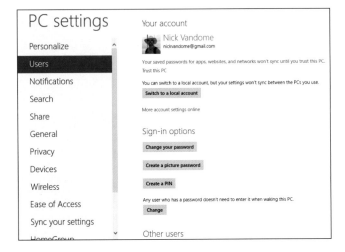

Notifications settings

Select the **Notifications** button to select options for the apps for which you will receive notifications. These will appear on the app tiles and some will also appear in pop-up boxes on the Start screen. They include new emails and messages and updated news items. Drag these buttons to turn the notifications On or Off.

Search settings

Select the **Search** button to select which apps you would like to use for searching items over. For instance, using search over the Internet Explorer app means that you will be able to search over the web with this function.

Share settings

Select the **Share** button to select options for how content is shared between apps. If the apps for sharing are turned Off then you will not be able to share content, such as photos, with these apps.

General settings

Select the **General** button to select options for the location of the time for your PC, allowing switching between apps (as shown on page 29), autocorrect for misspelled words, the language for input devices, refreshing your whole PC for improved performance, reinstalling Windows and the Advanced startup.

Don't forget

The date and time can be set within the Clock, Language, and Region section of the Control Panel, under the Date and Time heading.

PC settings	Time
Personalize	12:30, 03 September 2012
	(UTC-08:00) Pacific Time (US & Canada)
Users	Adjust for daylight saving time automatically
	On
Notifications	
Search	App switching
	Allow switching between recent apps
Share	On
General	When I swipe in from the left edge, switch directly to my most recent app
	On
Privacy	Delete history
Devices	
	Spelling
Wireless	Autocorrect misspelled words
Ease of Access	On
	Highlight misspelled words
Sync your settings	On
HomeGroup	

Privacy settings

Select the **Privacy** button to select options for letting apps use your geographical location over the Internet and also let them access your account username and picture. There is also an option for sending information to the Windows Store about the web content that your apps use.

PC settings	Privacy
	Let apps use my location
Search	On
Share	Let apps use my name and account picture
	On
General	Help improve Windows Store by sending URLs for the web content that apps use
Privacy	On
Devices	Privacy statement

Devices settings

Select the **Devices** button to add new devices such as printers. Click or tap on the **Add a device** button to start the process (see pages 56–57 for more details).

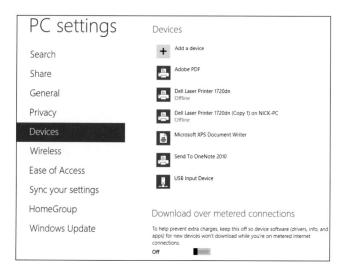

Devices should be switched on and connected to your PC or network in order for them to be found and then added.

Wireless settings

Select the **Wireless** button to select options for Airplane mode to stop wireless communications and to turn Wi-Fi on your computer On or Off.

...cont'd

Ease of Access settings

Select the **Ease of Access** button to select options for making the PC easier to use for people with visual or mobility issues. This includes the contrast of the screen, the size of everything on the screen (images and text) and options for turning on the Magnifier, Narrator and On-Screen Keyboard.

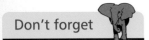

Don't forget

See Chapter Five for more information about the Ease of Access settings and options.

PC settings — Ease of Access

High contrast — Off

Make everything on your screen bigger — Off

Tab through webpages and apps using caret browsing — Off

Pressing Windows + Volume Up will turn on — Narrator

Show notifications for — 5 seconds

Cursor thickness — 1

Search / Share / General / Privacy / Devices / Wireless / Ease of Access / Sync your settings

Beware

Sync settings can only be changed if you are logged in with a Microsoft Account.

44

Sync your settings

Select the **Sync your settings** button to select options for syncing items that can then be used when you access your Microsoft Account from another online device.

Hot tip

Click or tap on the **Trust this PC** link under passwords so that you can use your passwords to access your settings from other computers.

PC settings — Sync your settings

Sync settings on this PC — On

Settings to sync

Personalize — Colors, background, lock screen, and your account picture — On

Desktop personalization — Themes, taskbar, high contrast, and more — On

Passwords — Your passwords won't sync until you trust this PC. Trust this PC

Sign-in info for some apps, websites, networks, and HomeGroup — On

Ease of Access — Narrator, Magnifier, and more — On

Language preferences — Keyboards, other input methods, display language, and more — On

App settings — Certain app settings and purchases made in an app

Search / Share / General / Privacy / Devices / Wireless / Ease of Access / Sync your settings / HomeGroup / Windows Update

HomeGroup settings

Select the **HomeGroup** button to select options for creating a HomeGroup for sharing your files with another Windows 8 PC. In this section there is a codeword that can be entered into the other PC to access your HomeGroup. (See Chapter 11 for more details about HomeGroups.)

Don't forget

Computers using Windows 7 can also be used to connect to a HomeGroup on a Windows 8 computer.

Windows Update settings

Select the **Windows Update** button to select options for how updates to Windows 8 are handled by your PC. By default, they are set to be installed automatically.

45

Organizing the Start Screen

By default, the new Windows 8 apps are organized into two groups on the Start screen. These are mainly the communication and information apps in the left-hand group and the entertainment apps in the right-hand group. However, it is possible to fully-customize the way that the apps are organized on the Start screen. To do this:

1. Move the cursor over the bottom right-hand corner and click or tap on this button to minimize the groups on the Start screen

2   Right-click on a group to select it. A tick will appear in the top right-hand corner to indicate that the group is selected

3   Drag the group to move its position on the Start screen

Moving tiles

Tiles can be rearranged within their respective groups. To do this:

1   Click, or press, and hold on a tile and drag it into a new position in the group

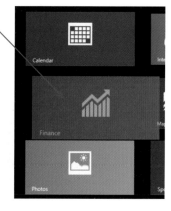

2   The other tiles move to accommodate the tile in its new position

...cont'd

Creating new groups

The two default groups of apps can be expanded by creating new groups from the existing ones. This is done by dragging the app tiles out of their current groups to create new ones. To do this:

1 Click, or tap, and hold on a tile and drag it away from its current group until a thick vertical line appears behind the tile

Don't forget

If a group is moved on the Start screen, its name moves with it.

48

2 Drag the tile into its new position to create a new group

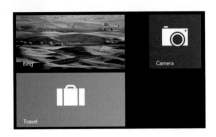

Resizing tiles

As well as rearranging tiles, their sizes can also be edited on the Start screen. Initially the tiles are a mixture of small and large sizes. However, the size of each tile can be changed. To do this:

1 Right-click on a tile to select it and click or tap on the **Smaller** button on the toolbar at the bottom of the screen

2 The tile is resized. If the tiles next to it are all larger then a space will appear next to the resized tile

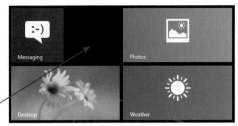

3 To enlarge a tile, right-click on it and click on the **Larger** button. If there is a space next to it, the resized tile will fill it. If there is no space then the other tiles will move to accommodate the new, larger, tile

Hot tip

From a design point of view it is a good idea to have a mixture of larger and smaller tiles on the Start screen.

49

4 If there are only smaller tiles after a larger tile, these will fill the space if the larger tile is made smaller as in Step 1

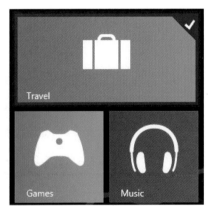

5 When the larger tile is reduced in size the next tile below it moves up automatically to fill in the space

Naming Groups

In their initial state, groups on the Start screen are not named, but it is possible to give them all their own individual names or titles. To do this:

1 Minimize the Start screen by moving the cursor over the bottom right-hand corner and clicking or tapping on this button

2 Right-click on a group so that a tick appears on it

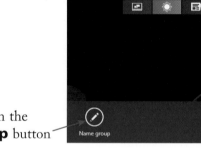

50

3 Click or tap on the **Name group** button

4 Enter a name for the group and click or tap on the **Name** button

Entertainment ✕

Name

Name group

5 The name is applied at the top of the group

Entertainment

Bing

Travel

Snapping

Although Windows 8 apps cannot be minimized in the traditional way, as with previous versions of Windows, there is a function that enables them to be "snapped" to the left or the right of the screen so that they are available when you are working in other apps. This takes effect in both the Windows 8 interface and the Desktop environment. To snap apps in this way:

1 Move the cursor over the top left-hand corner of the screen and drag down to view the currently-open apps

2 Click, or press, and hold on an app and drag it towards the main screen until a solid vertical bar appears (or swipe inwards slowly from the left-hand edge and drag one of the apps away from the App Switcher to snap it to the left-hand side)

3 Release the app and it will be snapped to the left-hand side of the screen

Beware

The snapping feature only works with a screen resolution of 1366 x 768 or above.

Don't forget

Click or tap on the thick border at the side of the snapped app to minimize this to a single bar. Click or tap on it again to maximize it.

Hot tip

To snap an app to the right-hand side, drag it across the screen to the right-hand border.

The Desktop

One of the first things you may say when you initially see Windows 8 is, "Where is the Desktop?" This is a fair question, given that the first thing you will see is the multi-colored Start screen. But the Desktop has not been removed: it is just sitting behind the Start screen. To access it:

1. On the Start screen, click or tap on the **Desktop** tile

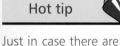

2. By default, the Taskbar at the bottom of the Desktop contains icons for Internet Explorer and File Explorer

3. Move the cursor over items on the Taskbar to see tooltips about the item. When apps are opened their icons appear on the Taskbar

4. The notifications area at the right-hand side of the Taskbar has speaker, network and other system tools. Click or tap on one to see more information about each item

The Control Panel

The Control Panel is a popular and valuable feature of Windows, but it may not be immediately obvious how to access it in Windows 8. There are a couple of ways to do this:

 On the Start screen, right-click and click or tap on the **All apps** button

All apps

 Scroll to the right and click or tap on the **Control Panel** button

Control Panel

or

 Right-click over the bottom left-hand corner of the screen and click or tap on the **Control Panel** link

Task Manager
Control Panel
Windows Explorer
Search
Run
Desktop

53

 Click or tap on the sections within the Control Panel to see more options for each and apply settings

Security Options

There are a number of security options that can be set within Windows 8 to help protect your computer from viruses or malicious software. These are accessed through the Action Center.

1 When there are important alerts, a red circle appears on the white flag in the notifications area on the Taskbar

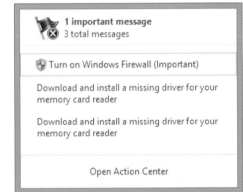

2 Click or tap the **flag** for brief details of the message(s), click or tap on a specific message or click or tap on the **Open Action Center** link

> 🏴 **1 important message**
> ⊗ 3 total messages
>
> 🛡 Turn on Windows Firewall (Important)
>
> Download and install a missing driver for your memory card reader
>
> Download and install a missing driver for your memory card reader
>
> Open Action Center

3 Security messages are color coded, with red being the most serious. Click on each item to undertake the required action to solve the problem

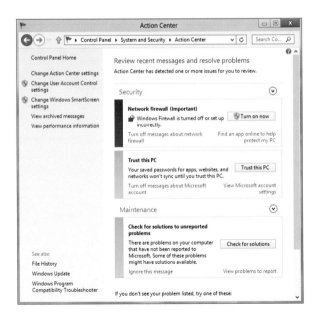

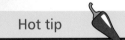

Don't forget

The Windows Firewall can help detect malicious software trying to access your computer. By default, this is on and should be left this way unless you have a specific reason to turn it off.

Hot tip

Some security issues have options for searching for apps online to help solve the problem.

54

Help and Support Center

Help is at hand for Windows 8 through the Help and Support Center and also online resources:

1 Move the cursor over the bottom right-hand corner of the screen and click or tap on the **Settings Charm**

2 Click or tap on the **Help** link under the Settings heading

Settings

Start

Tiles

Help

3 If the Help link is accessed in this way from the Start screen, this Help window is available. This takes you to online Help pages

⊖ Help

Adding apps, websites, and more to Start

Finding things with Search

Rearranging tiles on Start

Need more help?

Learn the basics:
Get started with Windows 8 and Start

Get support:
Visit the Windows website

4 If the Help link is accessed in this way from the Desktop, this Help window is available

Don't forget

Enter keywords into the Search box in Step 4 to look for specific items.

5 Click or tap on a link to view additional information about specific topics

Adding Devices

In most cases Windows will automatically install the software that will allow devices to work on your computer. However, on occasions you may have to do this manually, i.e. if you want to add a new printer to your PC. This can be done through the Hardware and Sound section in the Control Panel and the PC settings.

1 Connect the printer to the computer, either with a cable or wirelessly, and switch on the printer

2 Open the Control Panel and click or tap on the **View devices and printers** link under the Hardware and Sound heading

3 Click or tap on the **Add a printer** link at the top of the Devices and Printers window

4 Select the printer that you want to add and click or tap on the **Next** button

Don't forget

Printer drivers are small apps that enable printers to communicate with a computer and vice versa.

5 Select a driver for the printer and click or tap on the **Next** button

6 Select a name for the printer as required. This is what will appear when you select to print an item

7 If you would like other computers on the network to share the printer, click or tap on this button

8 Click or tap on the **Print a test page** button and click on the **Finish** button to complete adding the printer

Adding devices through PC settings

Devices such as printers can also be added through the PC settings of the Setting Charm.

1 Access the Settings Charm and click or tap on the **Change PC settings** button

Change PC settings

2 Click or tap on the **Devices** button

Devices

3 Click or tap on the **Add a device** button to add a new device

4 To delete a device, click or tap on it in the Devices section and click or tap on this button

5 Click or tap on the **Remove** button

Turning Off

To shut down your computer:

1 Move the cursor over the bottom right-hand corner of the screen (this can be done from either the Windows 8 interface or the Desktop, so the computer can be shut down from both environments)

2 Click or tap on the **Settings Charm**

3 Click or tap on the **Power** button

4 Click or tap on the **Shut down** or **Restart** options

Power saving options

You can also specify the action to be taken when you press the
hardware Power button.

1 Access the Control Panel,
Hardware and Sound
to view Power Options.
These vary between
laptops and desktops

2 You can select the
action to carry
out when you
press Power (or
Sleep or close the
lid for a laptop)

3 Select the
**Change when
the computer
sleeps**, option
in Step 1 to
apply settings for
what happens
after a period of
inactivity on the
computer, such
as dimming or
turning off the
screen display

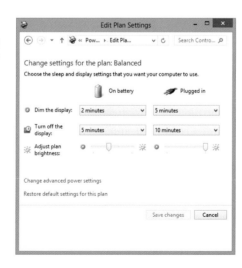

Don't forget

These options relate
to the physical power
button on the computer,
not to the on-screen
Power button.

Switching Users

If you have a number of user accounts defined on the computer (several accounts can be active at the same time) you do not need to close your apps and log off to be able to switch to another user and it is easy to switch back and forth.

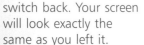
1 Click or tap on the name of the current active user in the top right-hand corner of the Start screen

2 Click on another user's name. They will have to enter their own password in order to access their account, at which point they will be signed in. You can then switch between users without each having to log out each time

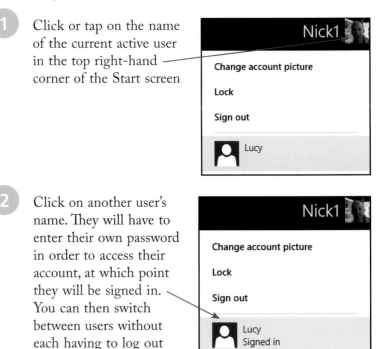

As an alternative way to switch users:

1 Press **WinKey** + **L**, to lock the current user

2 Access the login screen for all of the current users and select one as required

Shut Down

When you turn off your computer (see page 58), you will be warned if there are other user accounts still logged on to the computer.

Someone else is still using this PC. If you shut down now, they could lose unsaved work.

Shut down anyway

1 Click or tap on the **Shut down anyway** button to shut down without other users logging off

3 Working with Apps

"Apps" is one of the new buzzwords in computing. Put simply it is just another name for computer programs. In Windows 8, some apps are pre-installed, as with previous versions of Windows, while hundreds more can be downloaded from the Windows Store. This chapter shows how to work with and organize apps in Windows 8 and how to find your way around the Windows Store.

Starting with Apps

The word "app" may be seen by some as a new-fangled piece of techno-speak. But, simply, it means a computer program. Originally, apps were items that were downloaded to smartphones and tablet computers. However, the terminology has now been expanded to cover any computer program. So, in Windows 8 most programs are referred to as "apps", although some legacy ones may still be referred to as "programs."

There are three clear types of apps within Windows 8:

- New Windows 8 apps. These are the built-in apps that appear on the Start screen. They cover the areas of communication, entertainment and information and several of them are linked together through the online sharing service, SkyDrive

- Windows apps. These are the old-style Windows apps that people will be familiar with from previous versions of Windows. These open in the Desktop environment

- Windows Store apps. These are apps that can be downloaded from the online Windows Store, and cover a wide range of subjects and functionality. Some Windows Store apps are free while others have to be paid for

New Windows 8 apps

Windows 8 apps are accessed from the brightly colored tiles on the Start screen. Click or tap on a tile to open the relevant app:

Don't forget

The new Windows 8 apps open with the Windows 8 interface, rather than the more traditional Windows interface used with previous versions of Windows. However, the older Windows apps still use this interface.

Windows apps

The Windows apps are generally the ones that appeared as default with previous versions of Windows and would have been accessed from the Start Button. The Windows apps can be accessed from the Start screen by right-clicking on the screen and clicking on the **All apps** button on the bottom toolbar (see page 67 for more information). When Windows apps are opened from the Start screen they have the traditional Windows look and functionality. Windows apps open on the Desktop.

Don't forget

The **All apps** button can be accessed on a touch screen device by swiping up from the bottom of the Start screen. It can also be accessed by pressing **WinKey** + **Z** on a keyboard.

63

Windows Store apps

The Windows Store apps are accessed and downloaded from the online Windows Store. Apps can be browsed and searched for in the Store and when they are downloaded they are added to the Start screen.

Don't forget

The Windows Store is accessed by clicking or tapping on the **Store** tile on the Start screen.

Windows 8 Apps

The new Windows 8 apps that are accessed directly from the Start screen cover a range of communication, entertainment and information functions. The apps are:

 Calendar. This is an calendar which you can use to add appointments and important dates. It is closely integrated with the Mail, Messaging and People apps.

 Camera. This can be used to take photos directly onto your desktop, laptop or tablet computer, but only if it has an built-in camera attached.

 Desktop. Although this appears as an app on the Start screen, it takes you to the Desktop facility that has been available in previous versions of Windows.

 Finance. This is one of the information apps that provides real-time financial news. This is based on your location as entered when you installed Windows 8.

 Games. This can be used to play online Xbox games, either individually or by connecting to other online users and taking part in multi-player games.

 Internet Explorer. This is the Windows 8 version of the widely-used web browser. This version is IE 10 and the Windows 8 version has a different interface from the Desktop one.

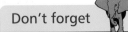 Mail. This is the online Mail facility. You can use it to connect to a selection of online Mail accounts (such as Outlook – previously Hotmail – and GMail) and send emails with photos and videos.

 Maps. This provides online access to maps from around the world. It enables locations to be viewed in Road or Aerial view and can also show traffic conditions for specific areas.

 Messaging. This is the online messaging service that can be used to send free text messages to other users with a compatible service. Messages can also include photos and videos.

Don't forget

See Chapter Nine for more information about working with Internet Explorer 10 in Windows 8 and Desktop mode.

Don't forget

See Chapter 10 for more information about working with the Calendar, Mail, Messaging and People apps and how content can be shared between the different apps.

Music. This can be used to access the online Music Store where music can be previewed and downloaded. It can be also used to organize and play the music on your computer.

 News. This is one of the information apps that provides real-time news information. This is based on your location as entered at installation.

 People. This is the address book app for adding contacts. Your contacts from sites such as Facebook and Twitter can also be imported into the People app.

 Photos. This can be used to view and organize your photos. You can also share and print photos directly from the Photos app.

 SkyDrive. This is an online facility for storing and sharing content from your computer. This includes photos, documents and your Mail, Calendar and People information.

 Sport. This is one of the information apps that provides real-time sports news. This is based on your location as entered when you installed Windows 8.

 Store. This provides access to the online Windows Store from where a range of other apps can be bought and downloaded to your computer.

 Travel. This is one of the information apps that provides travel news and features. This is based on your location as entered when you first installed Windows 8.

 Video. This can be used to access the online Video Store where videos can be previewed and downloaded. It can also be used to organize and play your videos.

 Weather. This provides real-time weather forecasts for locations around the world. By default it will provide the nearest forecast to your location as entered when you installed Windows 8.

 Don't forget

The information for the Finance, News, Sports and Travel apps is provided by Bing.

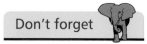 Don't forget

SkyDrive can also be used to share your content, such as photos and documents, with other people. See Chapter Eight for details.

Using Windows 8 Apps

The appearance of the new Windows 8 apps is different from those that have been provided with previous versions of Windows. Their functionality is slightly different too in that the toolbars and settings are hidden and only appear when required.

Accessing toolbars

To access toolbars in Windows 8 apps:

1. Right-click anywhere on the **app**

2. The toolbar appears at the bottom of the screen. This is relevant to the individual app. Therefore the toolbar will be different for the Photos and the Mail apps and so on

Accessing settings

Settings for individual Windows 8 apps can be accessed from the Settings Charm (the relevant app has to be the current one being used to view its settings):

1. Move the cursor over the bottom or top right-hand corner and click or tap on the **Settings Charm**

2. The settings options for the current app are displayed. Click or tap on each option to see the available settings

Don't forget

The bottom toolbar can be accessed on a touch screen device by swiping up from the bottom, or down from the top, of the screen in the relevant app. It can also be accessed by pressing **WinKey** + **Z** on a keyboard.

Beware

Always check at the top of the Settings panel to ensure that you have accessed the settings for the correct app.

Viewing All Apps

There is a lot more to Windows 8 than the default Windows 8 apps. Most of the system Windows apps that were available with previous versions of Windows are still here, just not initially visible on the Start screen. However, it is only takes two clicks on the Start screen to view all of the apps on your computer.

 Right-click anywhere on the **Start** screen

 Click or tap on the **All apps button** in the bottom right-hand corner

All of the apps are displayed. Scroll to the right to view all of the available apps

Click or tap on an app to open it

Don't forget

On a touch screen device, swipe up from the bottom, or down from the top, of the screen to view the **All apps** button.

Don't forget

Apps that are installed from a CD or DVD are automatically included on the Start screen, not just the All apps screen.

Beware

When you move away from the All apps screen the apps disappear from the Start screen. You have to access the **All apps** button each time you return to the Start screen and want to view the full range of apps.

Closing Windows 8 Apps

Because they have a different interface from traditional Windows apps, it is not always immediately obvious how to close a Windows 8 app. There are three ways in which this can be done:

Closing with the App Switcher sidebar

To close a Windows 8 app from the App Switcher sidebar:

 Move the cursor over the top left-hand corner of the screen and drag down to view all of the currently-open Windows 8 apps (see page 29)

2 Right-click on the app you want to close and click or tap on the **Close** button

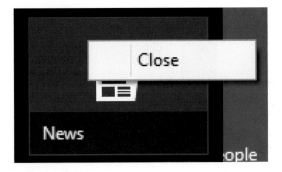

Don't forget

Any apps that open on the Desktop can still be closed in the traditional way of clicking or tapping on the cross at the top right-hand corner of the app.

Closing by dragging

To close a Windows 8 app by dragging it off the screen:

1 Move the cursor to the top of the screen until the pointer changes into a hand

2 Click, or tap, and hold at the top of the screen with the hand and drag down to the bottom of the screen

3 Release the mouse at the bottom of the screen and the app will disappear

Closing with the keyboard

To close a Windows 8 app by just using the keyboard:

1 With the current app active, press **Alt** + **F4**

Searching for Apps

As you acquire more and more apps, it may become harder to find the ones you want. To help with this you can use the Search Charm to search over all of the apps on your computer. To do this:

 Move the cursor over the top or bottom right-hand corner of the screen and select the **Search Charm**

Nick

Enter a word in the Search box and select **Apps** from the list below the Search box

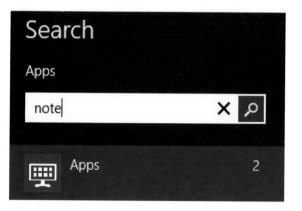

Search

Apps

note   ✕ 🔍

⌨ Apps   2

Hot tip

You just have to put in the first couple of letters of an app and Search will automatically suggest results based on this. The more that you type, the more specific the results become. Case does not matter when you are typing a search.

As you type, relevant apps are displayed. When the one you are seeking appears, click or tap on it to start the app

Apps   Results for " note "

Notepad

Sticky Notes

Pin to Start Screen

In most cases you will want to have quick access to a variety of apps on the Start screen, not just the new Windows 8 apps. It is possible to pin any app to the Start screen so that it is always readily available. To do this:

1 Access **All apps** (as shown on page 67)

(as shown on page 67)

2 Right-click on an app to select it, so that there is a tick showing in the top right-hand corner

3 When the app is selected the bottom toolbar appears. Click or tap on the **Pin to Start** button

4 The app is pinned to the Start screen. It can now be repositioned, if required, as with any other app (see page 47)

(see page 47)

Pin to Taskbar

Since most of the Windows system apps open on the Desktop you may want to have quick access to them here. This can be done by pinning them to the Desktop Taskbar (the bar that appears along the bottom of the Desktop). To do this:

1 Access **All apps** (see page 67)

2 Right-click on an app to select it, so that there is a tick showing in the top right-hand corner

3 When the app is selected the bottom toolbar appears. Click or tap on the **Pin to taskbar** button

4 Open apps on the Taskbar can also be pinned here by right-clicking on them and selecting **Pin this app to the Taskbar**

5 Pinned items remain on the Taskbar even once they have been closed

Hot tip

Apps can be unpinned from the Taskbar by right-clicking on them and selecting **Unpin this program from taskbar** from the contextual menu that appears.

Using the Windows Store

The third category of apps that can be used with Windows 8 are those that are downloaded from the Windows Store. These cover a wide range of topics and it is an excellent way to add functionality to Windows 8. To use the Windows Store:

1. Click or tap on the **Store** tile on the Start screen

2. The currently-featured apps are displayed on the home screen

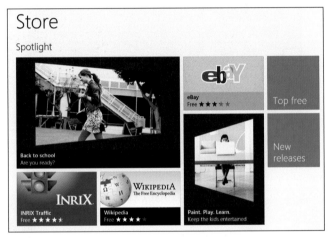

3. Scroll to the right to see additional categories of apps

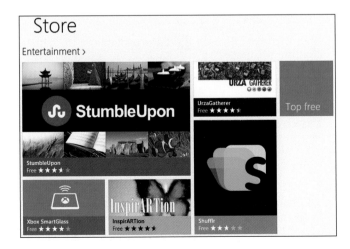

72

4 Click or tap on one of the green boxes to see the apps for that specific heading, i.e. Top free apps

5 The icons for the apps are displayed

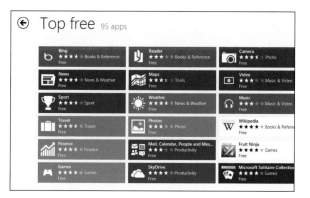

6 Click or tap on a category and select an app to preview

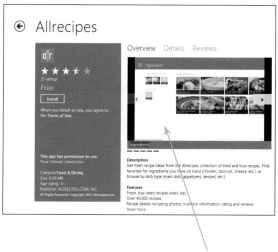

Don't forget

On the preview screen, click on the **Details** link to view details about the computer requirements for the app and the **Reviews** link to see what other people think.

7 Scroll here to preview additional pages about the app

...cont'd

8 Move the cursor over the bottom right-hand corner of the screen and click or tap here to minimize the app categories

9 Click or tap on a category to access it (it automatically enlarges on the screen from its minimized state)

10 Each category has options such as Top Free. If there are new releases for the category, these will be shown here

Buying Apps

When you find an app that you want to use you can download it to your computer or tablet. To do this:

1 Access the **Overview** screen for the app and click or tap on the **Install** button

2 To download apps from the Windows Store you need to have a Microsoft Account. Enter your details and click or tap on the **Sign in** button

3 The app is added to the Start screen and placed in the next space in the group to the furthest right on the Start screen

4 Click or tap on the app to open it and use it

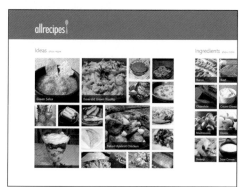

Viewing Your Apps

As you download more and more apps from the Windows Store you may lose track of which ones you have obtained and when. To help with this, you can review all of the apps you have downloaded, from within the Windows Store. To do this:

 Open the Windows Store and right-click anywhere on the **Home** screen

2 Click or tap on the **Your apps link** on the toolbar at the top of the screen

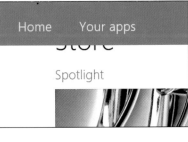

3 All of the apps you have downloaded are displayed, even if some have subsequently been uninstalled

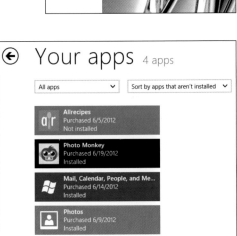

---

4 Click or tap on an app to select it

5 Use the buttons at the bottom of the screen to, from left to right, select all apps, clear a selection, install the selected app and view the details of the selected app

Using Live Tiles

Before any of the Windows 8 apps have been used, they are depicted on the Start screen with tiles of solid color. However, once you open an app it activates the Live Tile feature (if it is supported by that app). This enables the tile to display real-time information from the app, even when it is not the app currently being used. This means that you can view information from your apps, directly from the Start screen. To use Live Tiles:

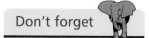

1 Right-click on a tile to select it. If it has Live Tile functionality, click or tap on the **Turn live tile on** button to activate this feature

Don't forget

The apps with Live Tile functionality include Mail, People, Messaging, Calendar, Photos, Music, News, Sport, Travel and Finance. Some of these, such as Mail and Messaging, require you to first set up an account before Live Tiles can be fully activated.

2 Live Tiles display real-time text and images from the selected apps. These are updated when there is new information available via the app

Beware

If you have too many Live Tiles activated at the same time it can become distracting and annoying, with a lot of movement on the Start screen.

3 To turn off a Live Tile, right-click on a tile to select it and click or tap on the **Turn live tile off** button

Apps on the Desktop

The Windows system apps open on the Desktop, in the same way as with previous versions of Windows, even though they are opened from the Start screen.

Opening a Windows system app

To open a Windows system app:

Don't forget

Windows system apps here refers to any apps that are not part of the Windows 8 interface. Within this group there are some apps known specifically as Windows System apps too.

1 Right-click on the Start screen and click or tap on the **All apps** button

All apps

2 Select the app you want to open

WordPad

3 The app opens on the Desktop

Hot tip

If apps have been pinned to the Taskbar, as shown on page 71, they can be opened directly from here by clicking or tapping on them.

4 Click or tap on the tabs at the top of the app to access relevant toolbars and menus

Closing a Windows system app

There are several ways to close a Windows system app:

1. Click or tap on the red **Close** button in the top right of the window

2. Select **File, Exit** from the File menu

3. Press **Alt**+**F4**

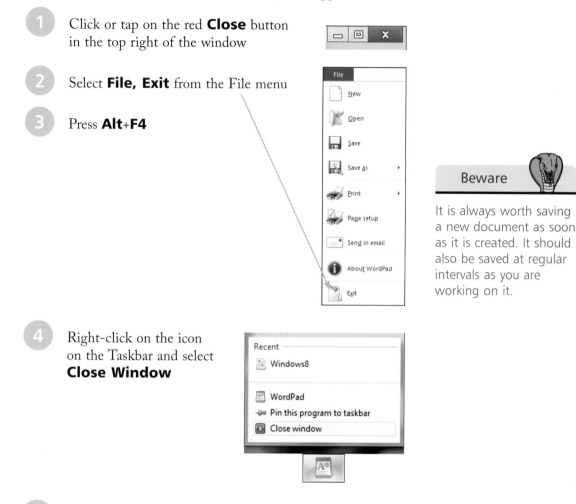

Beware

It is always worth saving a new document as soon as it is created. It should also be saved at regular intervals as you are working on it.

4. Right-click on the icon on the Taskbar and select **Close Window**

5. If any changes have been made to the document, you may receive a warning message advising you to save the associated file

Install and Uninstall

Installing apps from a CD or DVD

If the app you want to install is provided on a CD or DVD, you normally just insert the disc. The installation app starts up automatically and you can follow the instructions to select features and complete the installation.

If the installation does not start automatically, you can Run it from File Explorer by accessing the Setup.exe file. This should start the installation process To do this:

1   Right-click on the Start screen and click or tap on the **All apps** button

2   Select the **File Explorer** app

3   Access the CD or DVD in File Explorer

4   Access the **Setup.exe** file and double-click or tap on it to run it. Follow the onscreen prompts to install the app

5   Apps that are installed from a CD or DVD are automatically pinned to the Start screen

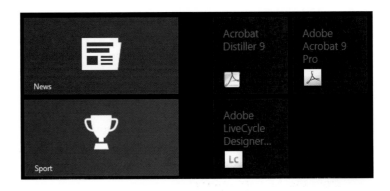

Uninstalling apps

In previous versions of Windows, apps were uninstalled through the Control Panel. However, in Windows 8 they can be uninstalled directly from the Start screen. To do this:

1 Right-click on an app to select it, as denoted by the tick in the top right-hand corner

Don't forget

If apps have been installed from a CD or DVD they can still also be uninstalled from within the Control Panel. To do this, select the Programs options and click on the **Uninstall a Program** link. The installed apps will be displayed. Select one of the apps and click on the **Uninstall/ Change** link.

2 Click or tap on the **Uninstall** button on the toolbar at the bottom of the screen

3 A window alerts you to the fact that related information will be removed if the app is uninstalled. Click or tap on the **Uninstall** button if you want to continue

This app and its related info will be removed from this PC.

 Allrecipes

Uninstall

Don't forget

Some elements of Windows 8, such as the Control Panel, still refer to apps as programs, but they are the same thing.

4 If the app is a new Windows 8 one, or has been pinned to the Start screen, its tile will be removed from the Start screen. For other apps, they will no longer be available from the All apps option

Task Manager

Task Manager lists all the apps and processes running on your computer; you can monitor performance or close an app that is no longer responding.

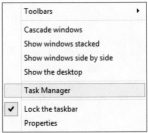

To open the Task Manager:

1 Right-click in the bottom left-hand corner and select **Task Manager**, or press **Ctrl + Shift + Esc**

2 When Task Manager opens, details of the currently-running apps are displayed

3 If an app is given the status of Not Responding and you cannot wait for Windows to fix things, select the app and click or tap on the **End task** button

4 Click or tap on the **More details** button to view detailed information about the running apps. Select the **Processes** tab to show the system and the current user processes

5 The total CPU usage and the amount being used by each process are shown as (continually varying) percentages

---

Don't forget

As an alternative, press **Ctrl + Alt + Delete** to display the Windows Security screen, from where you can start Task Manager.

82

Beware

If an app stops responding, Windows 8 will try to find the problem and fix it automatically. Using Task Manager to end the app may be quicker, but any unsaved data will be lost.

6 Select **Performance** to see graphs of resource usage

7 The Performance panel shows graphs of the recent history of CPU and memory usage, along with other details

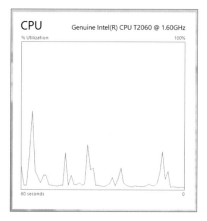

Alternative View

In addition to the standard view, with menus and tabs, Task Manager also has a CPU graph-only view.

1 To switch to the graph-only view double-click or tap the graph area on the Performance tab

2 To switch back to the view with menus and tabs, double-click or tap the graph area a second time

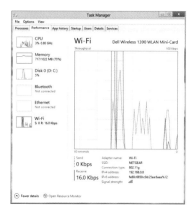

3 Select the **Wi-Fi** button in the Performance section to view the activity on your local area network. This tab also offers a graph-only view

Resource Monitor

The Resource Monitor provides an even more detailed view of the activities on your computer, and can be an essential aid in troubleshooting. To start the Resource Monitor:

1 From Task Manager, Performance tab Select the **Open Resource Monitor** button

Open Resource Monitor

2 This displays CPU, Memory, Disk and Network details

Right-click any process and choose **Analyze Wait Chain...** to see which tasks are holding up an unresponsive application.

| End Process |
| End Process Tree |
| Analyze Wait Chain... |
| Suspend Process |
| Resume Process |
| Search Online |

The Hardware Reserved section indicates how much of the 4 GB maximum memory is unavailable to applications. With the 64-bit Windows 8, most of this memory would become accessible.

3 For even more detail, select one of the tabs, e.g. Memory

4 Basic Controls

Even with the new Windows 8 interface, much of what you do in Windows 8 will be with menus, dialog boxes and windows. This chapter shows how to use these structures on the Desktop and how you can control working with folders and files.

Switching Windows

Hot tip

The contrast between the active window and the other windows is not very pronounced in the Windows 8 color scheme, but the red Close button helps:

If you have several windows open on your Desktop, one will be active. This will be the foremost window and it has its Title bar, Menu bar and outside window frame highlighted. If you have more than one window displayed on the Desktop, select anywhere inside a window that is not active to activate it and switch to it.

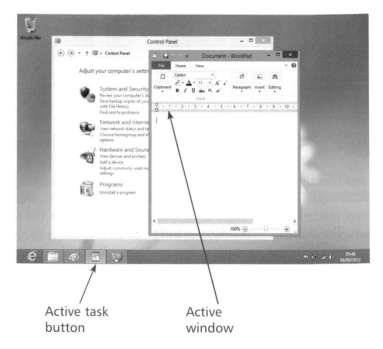

Active task button   Active window

Hot tip

If there is more than one window of the same type, then these tasks are grouped together on the Taskbar:

Another method of switching windows is to use the Taskbar at the bottom. Every window that is open has a button created automatically on the Taskbar. Therefore, it does not matter if the window you want to switch to is overlaid with others and you cannot see it. Just select the button for it in the Taskbar and the window will be moved to the front and made active.

Move the mouse pointer over a task button, and a live preview is displayed (one for each window if there are multiple tasks).

Don't forget

You can click or tap on the preview to select that task and bring its window to the front of the Desktop.

Arranging Icons

You can rearrange the order of the items in your folders or on your Desktop in many different ways.

 Right-click in a clear area (of the Desktop or folder window) to display a shortcut menu

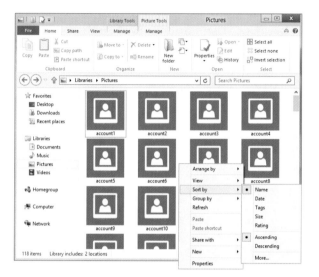

Hot tip

Select the **View** button to cycle through a range of views. Click, or tap, the **down arrow** to see the full set of options.

 Move the pointer over **Sort by**, to reveal the submenu of sorting options and click, or tap, e.g. the **Name** option, to sort all the file icons in ascending name order

Select **Name** a second time and the files will be sorted in descending name order

Group By

You can select **Group by** for folder windows (but not for the Desktop). This groups your files and folders alphabetically by name, size, type etc.

Closing a Window

When you have finished with a window you will need to close it. There are several ways of doing this – use the method that is easiest and the most appropriate at the time.

Open Window
If the top right corner of the window is visible on the Desktop:

1 Select the **Close** button on the Title bar

Minimized Window
For a window that is minimized or one that is hidden behind other windows:

1 Move the mouse pointer over the associated task button

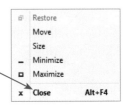

2 Select the **Close** button on the Live Preview for the task

Control Menu
If only part of the window is visible on the Desktop:

1 Select the **Control** icon (top left corner) or right-click the Title bar

2 Select **Close** on the Control menu

⊡	Restore	
	Move	
	Size	
—	Minimize	
❑	Maximize	
x	Close	Alt+F4

Keyboard
To close any type of window use this key combination.

1 Select the window to make it the current, active window, then press **Alt** + **F4** to close the window

---

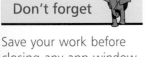

Don't forget

Save your work before closing any app window in which you have been working. However, Windows will prompt you if you forget.

Hot tip

Right-click the task button and select **Close** from the Jump List. If there are multiple tasks of the same type, the option offered is **Close all windows**.

 Close window

 Close all windows

5 Customizing Windows

The Desktop environment is still an important one in Windows 8 and this chapter looks at how to work with it and personalize it to your own requirements and preferences.

Personalize Your Desktop

As shown in Chapter Two there are plenty
of options for personalizing the Windows 8
interface. There are also a variety of options
within the Desktop environment too.

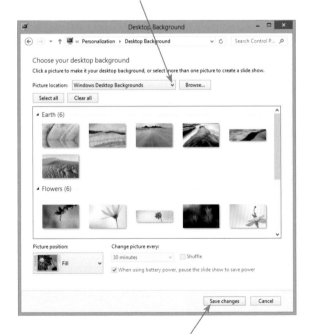

1 Right-click the Desktop and select
Personalize, or

2 Open the Control Panel and select **Appearance and
Personalization** and then select **Change desktop
background** under the Personalization option

Hot tip

Add a personal touch
to your computer by
taking advantage of the
flexibility in Windows,
and personalize settings
associated with your user
account name.

Don't forget

The functions offered
depend on the edition
of Windows 8 you
have installed and the
hardware specifications
of your computer.

3 Select a new **Desktop background**. Click or tap here
to access additional options

4 Click or tap on the Save changes button

5 The selected background is applied to the Desktop

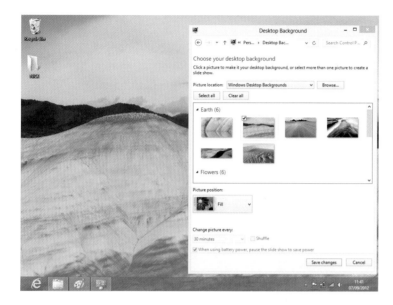

Don't forget

Personalization options allow you to change Desktop background, color, sound effects and screen saver, either individually, or all four at once by selecting a theme.

Don't forget

Click **Browse** to select your picture folder then select an image as background or a number of images as a slide show. You can change the timing and randomize the sequence.

Changing the theme

To change the overall theme of your Desktop, Taskbar and window borders:

1 Click or tap on the **Change the theme** link under the Personalization heading

Personalization
Change the theme | Change desktop background
Change the color of your taskbar and window borders
Change sound effects | Change screen saver

2 Select a theme in the same way as for selecting a Desktop background

3 Click or tap on this link on the themes page to obtain more from the Microsoft website

Get more themes online

Change Color and Sound

 Open Personalization and click the **Windows Color** button

 The available colors are displayed. The default color is located in the top left-hand corner

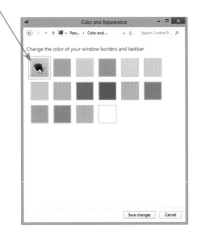

 Select a new color, which is applied to all window borders and the Taskbar

 Drag these sliders to edit the selected color

1 Select **Sounds** from Personalization, to see the name of the sound theme that gets applied to events in Windows

Sounds
Windows Default

A sound theme is a set of sounds applied to events in Windows and programs. You can select an existing scheme or save one you have modified.

Sound Scheme:

| Windows Default | ▼ | Save As... | Delete |

To change sounds, click a program event in the following list and then select a sound to apply. You can save the changes as a new sound scheme.

Program Events:

- 🔊 Windows
  - Asterisk
  - Calendar Reminder
  - Close Program
  - Critical Battery Alarm
  - Critical Stop

☐ Play Windows Startup sound

Sounds:

| (None) | ▼ | ▶ Test | Browse... |

OK Cancel Apply

Don't forget

Click or tap the down-arrow on the Sound Scheme bar to try out a different scheme.

2 Select a Program Event and click or tap the **Test** button to hear the associated sound

A sound theme is a set of sounds applied to events in Windows and programs. You can select an existing scheme or save one you have modified.

Sound Scheme:

| Windows Default (modified) | ▼ | Save As... | Delete |

To change sounds, click a program event in the following list and then select a sound to apply. You can save the changes as a new sound scheme.

Program Events:

- 🔊 Windows
  - Asterisk
  - Calendar Reminder
  - Close Program
  - Critical Battery Alarm
  - Critical Stop

☑ Play Windows Startup sound

Sounds:

| Windows Default | ▼ | ▶ Test | Browse... |

OK Cancel Apply

Hot tip

If you do not want to have sounds associated with Windows events, select **No Sounds**.

3 Browse to locate a new sound file (file type .wav), then select **Test** to preview the effect

4 Make any other changes, then select **Save As**, and provide a name for your modified sound scheme

Screen Saver

With the Screen Saver enabled, when your mouse or keyboard has been idle for a specified period of time, Windows 8 will display a moving image or pattern. To specify the image used:

1 From Personalization, select the **Screen Saver** button (which initially shows None)

2 Select the **Screen Saver** bar and choose a screen saver, e.g. Bubbles

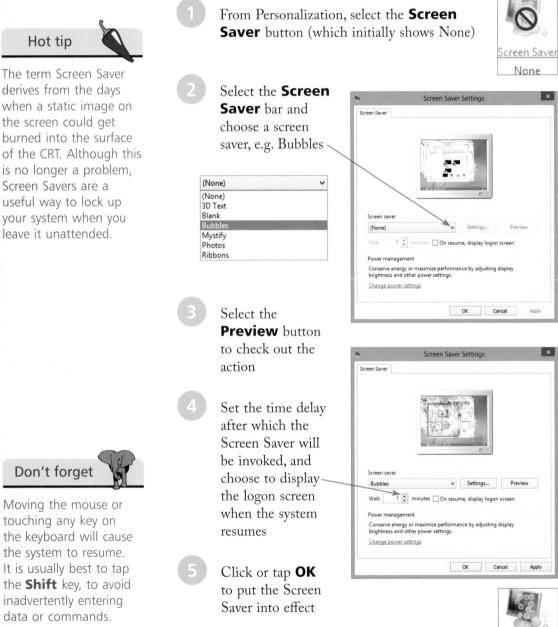

3 Select the **Preview** button to check out the action

4 Set the time delay after which the Screen Saver will be invoked, and choose to display the logon screen when the system resumes

5 Click or tap **OK** to put the Screen Saver into effect

Personalization will now show the name of the Screen Saver that has been enabled.

Desktop Icons

To control the display of icons on the Desktop:

1 Right-click on the Desktop, click or tap **View** and select **Show desktop icons**. A check mark is added

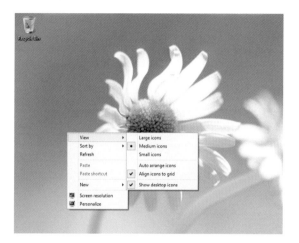

2 To resize the icons, display the View menu as above and click **Large icons**, **Medium icons** or **Small icons**

3 To remove the check mark and hide all the icons, display the View menu and select **Show desktop icons** again

4 To choose which of the system icons appear, open Personalization and select **Change desktop icons**

5 Select or clear the boxes to show or hide icons as required

Screen Resolution

If you have a high resolution screen, you may find that the text as well as the icons are too small. You can increase the effective size by reducing the screen resolution.

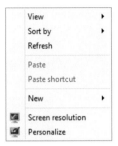

1 Right-click a clear section of Desktop and select **Screen resolution**

2 In the Control Panel, select **Appearance and Personalization** and select **Adjust screen resolution**

Don't forget

If you want to use the Snap function as shown in Chapter Two you need to have a minimum screen resolution of 1366 x 768.

Beware

If you have an LCD monitor or a laptop computer, you are recommended to stay with the native resolution, normally the highest. To resize text and icons in this case, you would adjust the DPI (see page 107).

3 Click or tap the down arrow next to Resolution and drag the slider, then click or tap **Apply**

4 Click or tap the down arrow next to Orientation to switch the view to **Portrait**, e.g. for tablet PCs

Display Settings

 Access the Control Panel and select **Appearance and Personalization** and then select **Display**

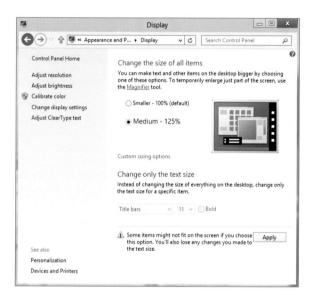

Don't forget

You can change your display settings and make it easier to read what is on the screen.

 Select, for example, **Medium – 125%**, and select **Apply**

Log off so that the change can take effect, then log on

Everything on the screen is increased in size if the display size is increased

Ease of Access Center

1 Open **Personalization** and select **Ease of Access Center**

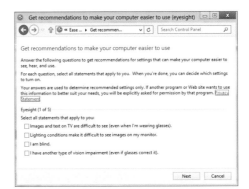

2 Click or tap on this bar to get recommendations on the settings that will be most appropriate for you

3 Otherwise, scroll down to explore all the settings. Those you select are started automatically each time you log on

For example, to use the Magnifier:

 Start Magnifier

1 Open the Ease of Access Center and select **Magnifier** (or press the Spacebar while Magnifier is highlighted)

2 Select the **Views** button on the Magnifier toolbar to choose **Full screen**, **Lens** or **Docked** operation

Hot tip

Move the mouse pointer over the Magnifying Glass and select it to display the Magnifier toolbar.

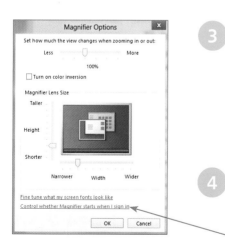

3 Select the **Options** button on the toolbar to specify the size of the Lens area, or to specify the tracking options for the other modes of operation

4 Select **Control whether Magnifier starts when I sign in**, to turn on Magnifier at start up

Don't forget

To stop using Magnifier during the session, right-click the Taskbar icon and select **Close Window**.

Date and Time Functions

To change the format Windows uses to display dates and times:

1 Access the Control Panel, and select **Clock, Language and Region**, and then the **Date and Time** option

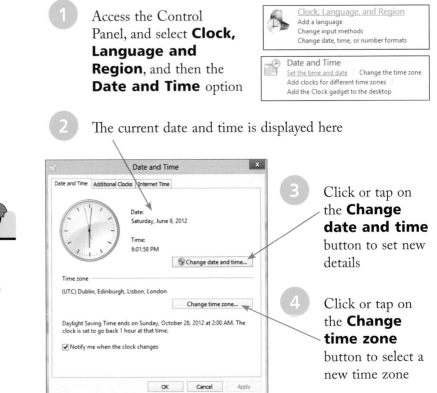

2 The current date and time is displayed here

3 Click or tap on the **Change date and time** button to set new details

4 Click or tap on the **Change time zone** button to select a new time zone

5 Click or tap on the **Region** option in Step 1 and click on the **Format** tab. This can be used to determine the way that time and dates are displayed

6 File Explorer

The File Explorer is at the heart of working with the files on your computer and you can use it to browse all of the information on your computer and on the local network. This chapter shows how you can use the Scenic Ribbon function, modify the views in File Explorer, sort the contents and customize the style and appearance.

Filtering

Hot tip

This shows ranges of values appropriate to the particular attribute and based on the actual contents of the folder. These ranges are used for filtering and for grouping the items in the folder.

Hot tip

Filtering can only be applied in the Details folder view.

Beware

If you navigate away from the folder or close File Explorer, the next time you visit the folder, the filtering will have been removed.

1 In the Details view, select any header and click or tap the **Down arrow**

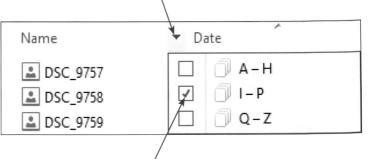

2 Select a box next to one or more ranges, and the items displayed are immediately restricted to that selection

3 You can select a second header, Size for example, to apply additional filtering to the items displayed

Size	▼	
2,310 K	☐	Small (10 - 100 KB)
2,718 K	☐	Medium (100 KB - 1 MB)
2,627 K	☐	Large (1 - 16 MB)

4 The tick ✓ symbol on headers indicates that filtering is in effect, and the Address bar shows the attributes

▸ Libraries ▸ Pictures ▸ Malawi ▸ I–P ▸ Medium (100 KB - 1 MB)   ∨ ᶜ Se

^ Name ✓ Date   Tags   Size   ✓

5 Filtering remains in effect even if you change folder views, within the selected folder

Grouping

You can group the contents of the folder using the header ranges. You do not need to select the Details view.

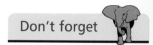
Don't forget

The right-click menu also offers the **Sort By** option, so you can specify or change the sort sequence without switching to Details view.

 1 Right-click an empty part of the folder area, move over **Group by**, then select an attribute, e.g. **Type**

2 The contents will be grouped, using the ranges for the attribute selected

Hot tip

Any sorting that was already in place will remain in effect. However, you can switch between **Ascending** and **Descending**.

3 Grouping is retained when you switch views (and when you revisit the folder after closing File Explorer)

Collapse Group

Hot tip

Select **Group By, (None)** to remove grouping. Select **More...** to add other attributes. The new attributes will also appear in Details view.

4 You can regroup the folder contents by selecting another attribute. This will replace your original choice

Folder Options

You can change the appearance and the behavior of your folders by adjusting the folder settings.

1 From the View tab in the Scenic Ribbon, click or tap on the **Options** button and select the **Change folder and search options** link

The same dialog box is displayed if you access the **Control Panel**, select **Appearance and Personalization**, then select **Folder** Options.

2 Choose **Open each folder in its own window**, to keep multiple folders open at the same time

Folder Options

General | View | Search

Browse folders
○ Open each folder in the same window
● Open each folder in its own window

Click items as follows
● Single-click to open an item (point to select)
  ○ Underline icon titles consistent with my browser
  ● Underline icon titles only when I point at them
○ Double-click to open an item (single-click to select)

Navigation pane
☑ Show favorites
☐ Show all folders
☐ Automatically expand to current folder

Restore Defaults

How do I change folder options?

OK | Cancel | Apply

Hot tip

To open a subfolder in its own window, when the **Open in same window option** is set, right-click the subfolder and select **Open in new window**.

3 If you want items to open as they do on a web page, select **Single-click to open an item (point to select)**

4 Select the **View** tab to select options for how items appear in the File Explorer libraries

5 Select **Apply** to try out the selected changes without closing the Folder Options

Apply

6 Select **Restore Defaults** then **Apply,** to reset all options to their default values

Restore Defaults

128

7 Managing Files & Folders

Folders can contain other folders as well as files, and Windows 8 treats them in very much the same way. Hence, operations such as moving, copying , deleting and searching apply to files and to folders in a similar way. This chapter shows how to perform these tasks and actions while working with folders and files within the File Explorer.

Select Files and Folders

Single File or Folder

Hot tip

To process several files or folders, it is more efficient to select and process them as a group, rather than one by one.

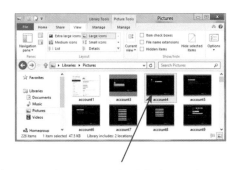

 Click or tap the item to highlight it, then move, copy or delete it as required

Sequential Files

Don't forget

Use the sorting, filtering and grouping options (see Chapter Six) to rearrange the files to make the selection easier.

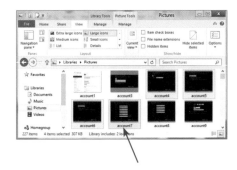

Click or tap to select the first item, press and hold **Shift**, then click or tap the last item, to highlight the range

Adjacent Block

Beware

You must start the box from an empty space in the folder. If you accidently click a file or folder, you will drag that item, rather than create a box.

Drag out a box to cover the files you want selected. All of the files in the rectangular area will be highlighted

Non-adjacent Files

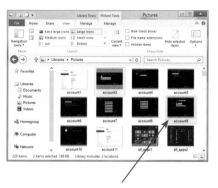

1. To select several, non-adjacent files, click or tap one item, press and hold **Ctrl**, then click or tap the subsequent items. As you select files, they are highlighted

Partial Sequence

You can combine these techniques to select part of a range.

1. Select a group of sequential files or an adjacent block of files (as described on page 130)

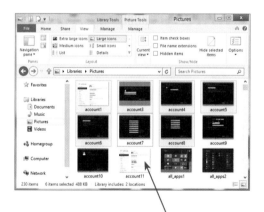

2. Hold down **Ctrl**, and click or tap to deselect any files in the range that you do not want and to select extra ones

All Files and Folders

To select all of the files (and folders) in the current folder, select the **Home** tab in the Scenic Ribbon and click or tap on **Select All** or press **Ctrl** + **A**.

Hot tip

To deselect one file, click it while the **Ctrl** key is being held down.
To deselect all of the files, click once anywhere in the folder outside the selection area.

Beware

If you select a folder, you will also be selecting any files and folders that it may contain.

131

Copy or Move Files or Folders

You may wish to copy or move some files and folders, to another folder on the same drive, or to another drive. There are several ways to achieve this.

Drag, Using the Right Mouse Button

1 Open File Explorer and the folder with the required files, then locate the destination in the Folders list

2 In the folder contents, select the files and folders that you want to copy or move

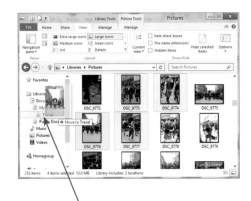

3 Right-click any one of the selection, drag the files onto the destination folder or drive in the Folders list, so it is highlighted and named, then release to display the menu

4 Click the **Move here** or **Copy here** option as desired, and the files will be added to the destination folder

Copy here
Move here
Create shortcuts here
Cancel

Drag, Using the Left Mouse Button

In this case default actions are applied, with no intervening menu.

 Select the files and folders to be moved or copied

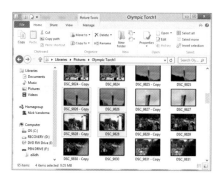

Open File Explorer and the source folder, then locate the destination in the folder list, ready for moving or copying files and folders.

2 Use the left mouse button to drag the selection to the destination drive or folder in the Folders list, in this example the removable USB storage drive

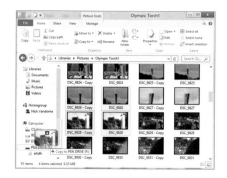

As you hover over a drive or folder in the Folders list, it expands to reveal the subfolders.

133

3 Press **Shift** to Move instead of Copy to another drive. Press **Ctrl** to Copy instead of Move to a folder on the same drive as the source folder

In Summary

Don't forget

You will see a ➕ symbol if the file is going to be copied, or a ➡ if the file is going to be moved.

Drives	Drag	Drag+Shift	Drag+Ctrl
Same	Move	Move	Copy
Different	Copy	Move	Copy

...cont'd

Using Cut, Copy, Paste

1 Choose the files and folders you want to copy and right-click within the selection

2 From the shortcut menu click or tap **Copy** or **Cut** to move the selection

3 Right-click and click or tap **Open in new windows,** for the folder in which you want to put the selection

4 Right-click a blank area of the destination folder

5 Select **Paste** from the menu to complete the Copy or move operation

Keyboard Shortcuts
Cut, Copy and Paste options are also available as keyboard shortcuts. Select files and folders as above, but use these keys in place of the menu selections for Copy, Cut and Paste. There are also shortcuts to Undo an action or Redo an action.

Press this key	To do this
F1	Display Help
Ctrl+C	Copy the selected item
Ctrl+X	Cut the selected item
Ctrl+V	Paste the selected item
Ctrl+Z	Undo an action
Ctrl+Y	Redo an action

Burn to Disc

If your computer has a CD or DVD recorder, you can copy files to a writable disc. This is usually termed "burning".

1 Insert a writable CD or DVD disc into the recorder drive (DVD/CD RW). Click or tap on this popup

2 When the prompt appears, choose the option to **Burn files to disc** using File Explorer

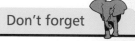

3 Amend the suggested disc title if desired

4 Choose how you plan to use the disc you will be creating and click or tap on the **Next** button. The disc will then be formatted

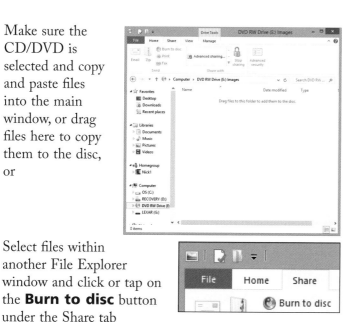

5 Make sure the CD/DVD is selected and copy and paste files into the main window, or drag files here to copy them to the disc, or

6 Select files within another File Explorer window and click or tap on the **Burn to disc** button under the Share tab

Don't forget

Select the **Like a USB flash drive** option in Step 4 if you want to be able to use the files on another computer. Select the With a CD/DVD player option if you want to use them in this way.

Don't forget

You can use any of the methods described for copying or moving one, or more, files and folders (see pages 132–134).

File Conflicts

When you copy or move files from one folder to another, conflicts may arise. There may already be a file with the same name in the destination folder. To illustrate what may happen:

1 Open the Pictures, Olympic Torch folder and the Backup folder

2 Press **Ctrl** + **A** to select all of the files and drag them onto the Backups folder, to initiate a copy of them

Hot tip

You can of course use the Copy and Paste options from the right-click menus, or use the equivalent keyboard shortcuts, and File Explorer will continue to check for possible conflicts.

3 Windows observes a conflict – this file already exists, with identical size and date information. Select one of the options

4 If you select the Compare info for both files, details will be displayed so you can view if one is newer than another. Click or tap on the **Continue** button to perform additional actions on the file

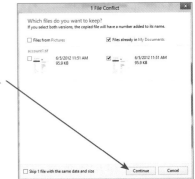

Open Files

You can open a file, using an associated app but without having first to explicitly start that app. There are several ways to do this:

Default Program

1 Double-click or tap the file icon

2 Right-click the file and select **Open** from the menu

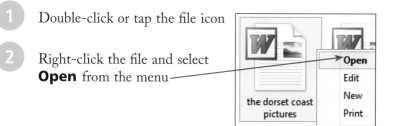

3 Select the file, then click or tap **Open** from the Home section of the Scenic Ribbon. This will open the file in its default app

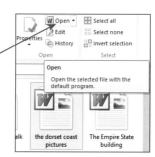

Alternative Program (App)

You may have several apps that can open a particular file type. To use a different app than the default to open the file:

1 Right-click the file icon and select **Open with**. Pick an app from the list or click **Choose default program** to set a new default app

2 The same choices are presented, when you select the down arrow next to the **Open** button on the Scenic Ribbon in the folder window

Delete Files and Folders

When you want to remove files or folders, you use the same delete procedures – whatever drive or device the items are stored on.

Don't forget

When you delete files and folders from your hard disk drive, they are actually moved to a temporary storage area, the Recycle Bin (see page 139).

1 Choose one or more files and folders, selected as described previously (see page 130)

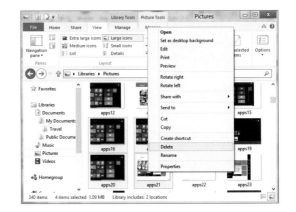

Hot tip

You can press the **Delete** key on your keyboard, after selecting the files and folders, instead of using the menus.

2 Right-click the selection and click **Delete**

3 Alternatively, click or tap on the **Delete** button on the Scenic Ribbon and click or tap on one of the options

Don't forget

You may need to have administrator authority to delete some files or folders from your system.

4 You get an **Are you sure?** message, whether there are multiple files or a single file involved. Select **Yes** to confirm, or **No** to cancel deletion

If you choose to delete then immediately realize that you have made a mistake deleting one or more files, right-click the folder area and select **Undo Delete** or press **Ctrl** + **Z**, to reverse the last operation. For hard disk items, you are also able to retrieve deleted files from the Recycle Bin, and this could be a substantial time later.

The Recycle Bin

The Recycle Bin is, in effect, a folder on your hard disk drive that holds deleted files and folders. They are not physically removed from your hard disk (unless you empty the Recycle Bin or delete specific items from within the Recycle Bin itself). They will remain there, until the Recycle Bin fills up, at which time the oldest deleted files may be finally removed.

The Recycle Bin, therefore, provides a safety net for files and folders you may delete by mistake and allows you to easily retrieve them, even at a later date.

Restoring Files

1 Double-click on the **Recycle Bin** icon from the Desktop or in the Computer folder

Don't forget

To see where the Recycle Bin is located, right-click the **Navigation pane** and select **Show all folders**.

2 Select the **Restore all items** button, or select a file and the button changes to **Restore this item**

Hot tip

A restored folder will include all the files and subfolders that it held when it was originally deleted.

Permanently Erase Files

You may want to explicitly delete particular files, perhaps for reasons of privacy and confidentiality.

1 Open the Recycle Bin

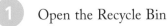

Don't forget

You do not have to worry about the space used in the Recycle Bin. Windows keeps track and removes the oldest deleted entries when the maximum allowed space, typically 10% of the drive, has been used.

2 Select the relevant files and folders, then select **Delete** from the one of the menus (or press the **Delete** key)

3 Select **Yes**, to confirm that you want to permanently delete these files (completely remove from the hard disk)

Empty the Recycle Bin

If desired, you can remove all of the contents of the Recycle Bin from the hard disk.

Hot tip

Right-click the Recycle Bin icon and select **Empty Recycle Bin**, to remove all of the files and folders without it being open.

1 With the Recycle Bin open, select the **Empty Recycle Bin** button

2 Press **Yes** to confirm the permanent deletion

The Recycle Bin icon changes from full to empty, to illustrate the change.

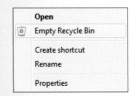

Bypass the Recycle Bin

If you want to prevent particular deleted files from being stored in the Recycle Bin:

 Select the files and folders, right-click the selection but this time, hold down the **Shift** key as you select **Delete**

Hot tip

You could also just press the **Delete** key on the keyboard to delete items.

2 Confirm that you want to permanently delete the selected item or items. "Permanent" means that no copy will be kept

Beware

Take extra care when selecting files and folders, if you are bypassing the Recycle Bin, since you will have no recovery options.

Deactivate (or Resize) the Recycle Bin

You can tell Windows to always bypass the Recycle Bin.

1 Right-click the Recycle Bin icon, then select **Properties** from the menu

2 Note the space available on Recycle Bin location (free space on hard disk)

3 Adjust the maximum size allowed, to resize the Recycle Bin

Don't forget

This dialog box also allows you to suppress the warning message issued when you delete items.

4 Click or tap the button labeled **Don't move files to the Recycle Bin. Remove files immediately when deleted**, to always bypass the Recycle Bin

Create a File or Folder

You can create a new folder in a drive, folder or on the Desktop.

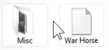
1 Right-click an empty part of the folder window and select **New** and then **Folder**

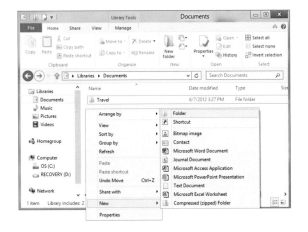

2 Overtype the default name New Folder, e.g. type *Articles*, and press **Enter**

To create a new file in a standard format for use with one of the apps installed on your computer.

1 Right-click an empty part of the folder, select **New**, and choose the specific file type e.g. Rich Text File document

2 Overtype the file name provided and press **Enter**

Genealogy Today

New Rich Text Document

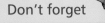

Rename a File or Folder

You can rename a file or folder at any time, by simply editing the current name.

1 Right-click the file/folder, then click **Rename**, or select the icon and click or tap on the icon name

2 Either way, the current name will be highlighted. Type a name to delete and replace the current name; or press the arrow keys to position the typing cursor and edit the existing name:

3 Press **Enter** or click or tap elsewhere to confirm the name

Preserving File Types

When you have file extensions revealed and you create or rename a file or folder, only the name itself, not the file type, will be highlighted. This avoids accidental changes of type.

Hot tip

Use the same method to rename icons on the Desktop. You can even rename the Recycle Bin.

Don't forget

You must always provide a non-blank file name, and you should avoid special characters such as quote marks, question marks and periods.

143

Beware

You can change the file type (extension), but you will be warned that this may make the file unusable.

Backtrack File Operations

If you accidentally delete, rename, copy or move the wrong file or folder, you can undo (reverse) the last operation and preceding operations, to get back to where you started. For example:

1 Right-click the folder area and select the **Undo Rename** command that is displayed

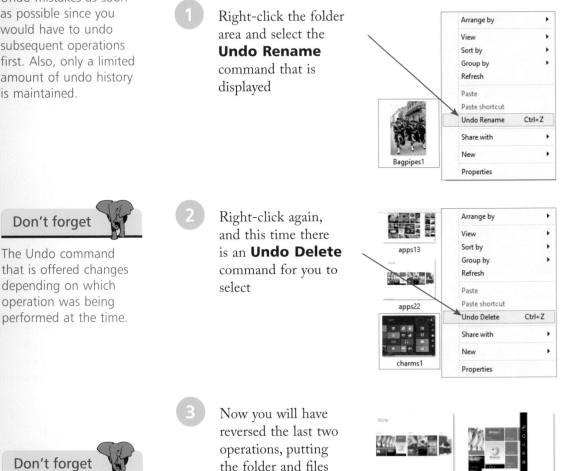

Arrange by	▶
View	▶
Sort by	▶
Group by	▶
Refresh	
Paste	
Paste shortcut	
Undo Rename	Ctrl+Z
Share with	▶
New	▶
Properties	

Bagpipes1

2 Right-click again, and this time there is an **Undo Delete** command for you to select

apps13

apps22

Arrange by	▶
View	▶
Sort by	▶
Group by	▶
Refresh	
Paste	
Paste shortcut	
Undo Delete	Ctrl+Z
Share with	▶
New	▶
Properties	

charms1

3 Now you will have reversed the last two operations, putting the folder and files back as they were before the changes

apps22   apps23

Band1   charms1

File Properties

Every file (and every folder) has information that can be displayed in the Properties dialog box. To display this:

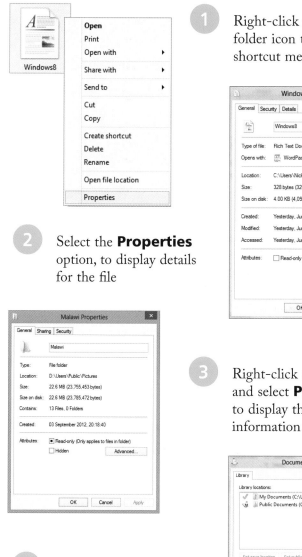

1 Right-click the file or folder icon to display the shortcut menu

2 Select the **Properties** option, to display details for the file

3 Right-click a folder icon and select **Properties**, to display the folder information

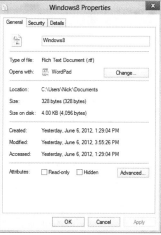

4 You can similarly display Properties for any of the Libraries

Hot tip

The purpose of the Properties dialog box is:
• to display details
• to change settings for the selected file or folder.

Don't forget

Click **Security** and other tabs, to display more information about the file or folder, and click the **Advanced** button for additional attributes.

Hot tip

In View mode on the Scenic Ribbon, select a folder and select the **Options** button. Then select the **Change folder and search options** link to view folder properties.

Search for Files and Folders

If you are not quite sure where exactly you stored a file, or what the full name is, the File Explorer Search box may be the answer.

1 Open a location, e.g. Documents, click or tap in the Search box and start typing a word from the file, e.g. Nick

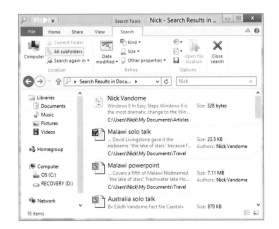

2 If that produces too many files, start typing another word that might help limit the number of matches, e.g. *Vandome*

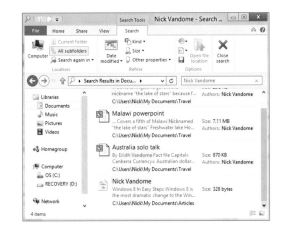

3 If the location is a drive rather than a library, its contents may not be indexed, so the search may take longer

Compressed Folders

This feature allows you to save disk space by compressing files and folders while allowing them to be treated as normal by Windows 8.

Create a Compressed Folder

 Right-click an empty portion of the folder window and select **New > Compressed (zipped) Folder**

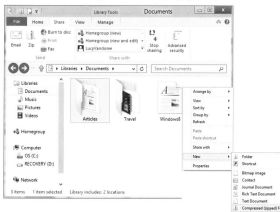

 A compressed folder is created, with default name New Compressed (zipped) Folder.zip

Rename it (see page 143). You can also open, move, or delete it just like any folder

Add Files or Folders to a Compressed Folder

Drag files or folders onto a compressed folder and they will automatically be compressed and stored there

Hot tip

Compressed folders are distinguished from other folders by a zipper on the folder icon. They are compatible with other zip archive apps, such as Winzip.

Don't forget

To create a compressed folder and copy a file into it at the same time: right-click a file, select **Send To, Compressed (zipped) Folder**. The new compressed folder has the same file name, but a file extension of .zip.

Hot tip

The compressed folder is treated like a separate device. By default, files will be copied rather than moved when they are dragged to, or from, the folder.

Compressed Item Properties

 Double-click the compressed folder and select any file to see the compressed size versus the actual size

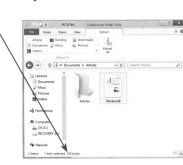

Extract Files and Folders

Open the compressed folder, drag files and folders onto a normal folder and they will be decompressed. The compressed version still remains in the compressed folder, unless you hold the **Shift** key as you drag (i.e. Move)

Extract All

To extract all of the files and folders from a compressed folder, right-click it and then click on **Extract All**

Extract all

Accept or edit the target folder and click **Extract**. The files and folders are decompressed and transferred

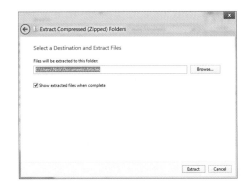

Fonts Folder

Windows includes several hundred different fonts. These offer a wide range of distinctive and artistic effects in windows and documents, and support multiple languages and special symbols.

To view the fonts available on your system:

1 Access the Control Panel and open **Fonts** from **Appearance and Personalization**

2 The Fonts folder is displayed in File Explorer

3 Double-click or tap on a group font such as Calibri to see the font styles that it contains

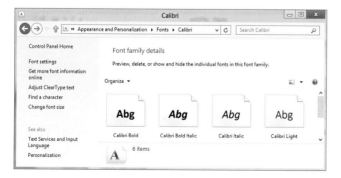

149

Don't forget

You can also find the Fonts folder within the C:\Windows folder.

Hot tip

Double-click or tap on a font to see samples of the characters at various point sizes.

Hot tip

Most of the Windows fonts will be TrueType or OpenType fonts which can be scaled to any size and can be sent to any printer or other output device that is supported by Windows.

Character Map

As well as letters and numbers, the fonts contain many special characters, not all of which appear on your computer keyboard. You can insert these characters into your documents using the Character Map, or by pressing particular key combinations.

1 In the Fonts folder select **Find a character** to display the Character Map application

Find a character

Change font size

150

2 Select any character to see an enlarged version. The key combination and description is shown on the status bar

3 Click or tap **Select** to add the character to the copy box, and click or tap **Copy** to transfer it to the clipboard

Characters to copy : ©   Select   Copy

4 Click or tap the Font box to select a different font from the list, for example Wingdings

8 Digital Lifestyle

Windows 8 makes it easy to work with digital media with the new Photo, Music, Video and Games apps. This chapter shows how to work with these apps so that you can fully immerse yourself in the digital world.

Playing Games

The Games app can be used with the Xbox 360 games console. It can be used to play games, join friends for multi-player games, watch TV shows and movies and listen to music. It links into a number of services so that you can access content from websites such as YouTube and Netflix. To use the Games app:

1. Click or tap on the **Games** tile on the Start screen

2. You have to log in with your Microsoft Account details. Enter these and click or tap on the **Continue** button

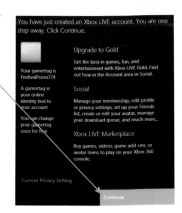

Don't forget

When you first log in to the Games app you will be given a gametag, which will be used to identify you on the Xbox games site.

3. Click or tap on a game to preview it and play it

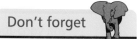

Hot tip

You can also log in to the Xbox site at www.xbox.com to download games and find other people with which to play games.

4. The Xbox website gives you access to a range of additional content

Sharing with SkyDrive

Cloud computing is now a mainstream part of our online experience. This involves saving content to an online server connected to the service that you are using, i.e. through your Microsoft Account. You can then access this content from any computer, using your account login details, and also share it with other people by giving them access to your cloud service. It can also be used to back up your files, in case they are corrupted or damaged on your PC.

The cloud service with Windows 8 is known as SkyDrive and you can use it providing that you have a Microsoft Account.

1 Click or tap on the **SkyDrive** tile on the Start screen

2 The SkyDrive folders are displayed. Click or tap on one to view its contents, or add files

3 Right-click or drag up from the bottom of the screen to view the SkyDrive toolbar at the bottom of the screen

Don't forget

Items can be shared with Windows and Mac users.

4 Click or tap on the **Upload** button to add files to the active folder

...cont'd

5 Navigate to the files that you want to add to SkyDrive and click or tap on them to select them

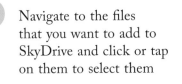

6 Click or tap on this button

7 The selected files are added to the active SkyDrive folder

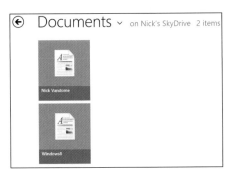

Sharing with SkyDrive

To share files from SkyDrive:

1 Access the **Share Charm**

2 Select items by right-clicking on them. Select a method for sharing, such as **Mail** for sending an email

3 The email contains a link to the SkyDrive folder. The recipient will be able to use this to access the folder and download the items within it

9 Internet Explorer 10

Internet Explorer, the widely-used Microsoft web browser, has been redesigned for Windows 8 and the latest version, IE 10, can be used with different interfaces whether it is in Windows 8 mode or the traditional Desktop mode. This chapter looks at the difference between the two, introduces the new features of the Windows 8 version and shows how to use the Share, Search and Print Charms to transform your online web browsing experience.

Internet Connection

Hot tip

Most ISPs also provide additional services such as email accounts, web servers and storage space on their Internet servers for you to create your own website.

Don't forget

It is usually better to use the software and procedures offered by your ISP, if possible, since they will be specifically tailored for the particular service.

Before you can use the Internet and browse the web, your computer needs to be set up for connection to the Internet. To do this you'll require:

- An Internet Service Provider (ISP), to provide an account that gives you access to the Internet

- A transmission network – cable, telephone or wireless

- Some hardware to link into that transmission network

- For a broadband connection, such as Digital Subscriber Line (DSL) or cable, you need a DSL or Cable modem or router, usually provided by the ISP

- For dial-up connection, you need a dial-up modem, which is usually pre-installed on your computer

Your ISP may provide software to help you set up your hardware, configure your system and register your ISP account details. However, if you are required to install the connection or, if you are configuring a second connection as a backup, you can use the Set Up a Connection or Network wizard.

1. Access the **Control Panel** and select the **View network status and tasks** link, under the Network and Internet heading. This opens in the Network and Sharing Center

2. Click or tap on **Setup a new connection or network** link to display the connection options supported

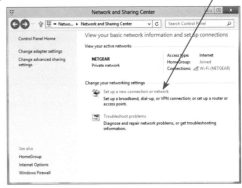

3 Select **Connect to the Internet** and click or tap **Next**

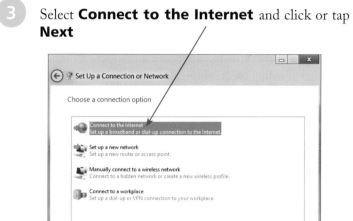

4 The Connect to the Internet wizard launches. Select the appropriate connection method from those offered

Windows identifies all of the possible connection methods based on the hardware configuration of your computer. If you have a wireless router or network, you may have an option for Wireless connection. If there is no dial-up modem installed, then the Dial-up connection method will not be offered.

Beware

If Windows has already recognized your connection, it detects this. You can select **Browse the Internet now** or **set up a second connection** (e.g. as a backup).

Don't forget

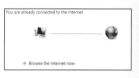

Continue through the wizard to complete the definition of your Internet connection, ready to start browsing the Internet.

IE 10 in Windows 8 Mode

The default web browser, for connecting to the World Wide Web (WWW), provided with Windows 8 is Internet Explorer (IE) 10. However, there is a slight twist as it is a two-for-one browser in many respects: there is one version for the new Windows 8 interface and another Desktop version which will be more familiar to anyone who has used previous versions of IE.

IE 10 for Windows 8 mode is optimized to display the maximum amount of screen estate, without a lot of clutter in terms of toolbars. It is also designed for touch screen use, although you can use it perfectly well by using a mouse and keyboard too.

1 To open the new Windows 8 version of IE 10, click or tap on this tile on the Start screen

2 The IE 10 toolbars are hidden so that the web pages can be viewed with the whole screen

3 Right-click on the screen, or swipe down from the top or up from the bottom of the screen, to access the Tab Switcher at the top of the screen

and the Navigation Bar at the bottom. Click or tap once on the screen or swipe upwards on the Tab Switcher to hide these items

Opening Pages

The Navigation Bar that can be accessed at the bottom of the screen (see page 170) can be used to open new web pages.

1 Type a web address in the Address Bar. When you click or tap in the Address Bar, icons of the pages that you have visited are available. Click or tap on one to open it

2 As you start typing a web address in the Address Bar, suggestions appear above it. These change as you add more letters in the Address Bar. Click or tap on one of the suggestions if you want to open that page

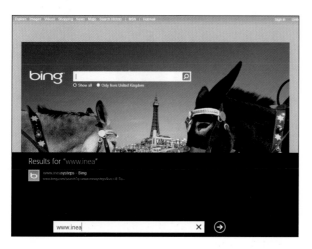

Hot tip

If you are entering a web address into IE 10 you do not require the initial www: as you start typing the address, suggestions will appear.

Navigating Pages

Because of the simplified interface for IE 10 in Windows 8 mode there is not the range of functionality of the Desktop version. However, this also means that pages can be navigated around quickly and efficiently with a few clicks or taps.

Don't forget

When you hover over a link in IE 10 in Windows 8 mode, the link to the associated page is shown in a tooltip box at the bottom of the screen.

Hot tip

If you are viewing IE 10 in Windows 8 mode on a touch screen device you can zoom in on a web page by pinching outwards with two fingers. Pinch inwards to zoom out.

1 Use these buttons on the Navigation Bar at the bottom of the screen to, from left to right, refresh/stop the current page, pin the page to the Start screen and access page tools

2 When moving between different web pages, move the cursor over the left edge and click or tap on the **Back arrow**. Do the same at the opposite side of the screen for the **Forward** button

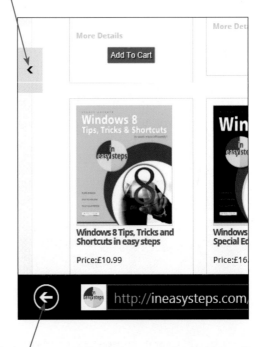

3 Click or tap on this button on the Address Bar for the Back function (the **Forward** button is on the other side)

Pinning a Web Page

If you have favorite web pages that you visit often it can be frustrating having to access them through IE 10 each time, even with the frequently-visited pages as shown on page 171.
A solution to this is to pin a link to the Start screen. This means that you can access the page directly from the Start screen; IE 10 will be opened at the selected page. To pin a web page:

1 Open the required web page and click or tap on this button on the Address Bar

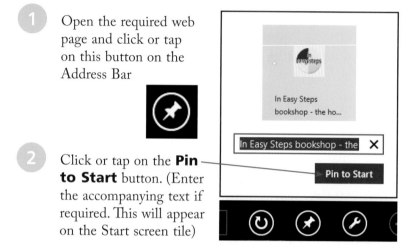

2 Click or tap on the **Pin to Start** button. (Enter the accompanying text if required. This will appear on the Start screen tile)

Don't forget

Access the IE 10 Address Bar by right-clicking on a web page or swiping up from the bottom, or down from the top, of the screen.

3 The link to the page is added to the Start screen as a new tile. Click or tap on this to open the page directly

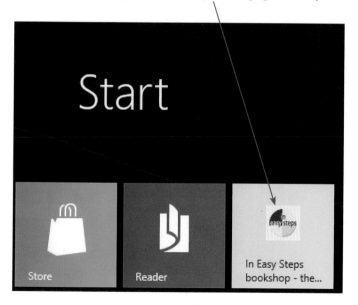

Tabs in Windows 8 Mode

Tabs within web browsers are now an established part of our online experience. This enables multiple web pages to be open in the same window. Each tab can have its own content displayed. In IE 10 in Windows 8 mode, tabs are accommodated by the Tab Switcher that is accessed at the top of the screen by right-clicking on the main screen, or dragging down from the top of the screen on a touch screen device. To work with tabs in IE 10 Windows 8:

1 Click or tap on this button at the top right-hand corner of the Tab Switcher to add a new tab

2 Open a web page in the regular way

3 The open tabs are displayed on the Tab Switcher. Click or tap on a tab to access that page. Click or tap on the cross on the tab thumbnail to close a tab

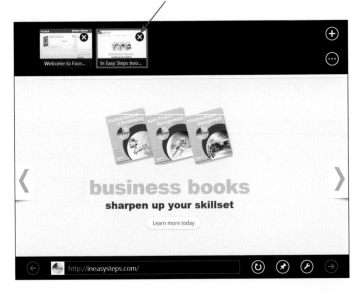

Beware

InPrivate browsing leaves no record of the browser session, in terms of pages visited. Therefore it is not a good option if children are using it.

4 Click or tap on this button to open an InPrivate Browsing tab or close all of the currently-open tabs

IE 10 Windows 8 Settings

As with other Windows 8 apps, IE 10 in Windows 8 mode has its own settings which are accessed from the Settings Charm.

1 Open a web page in IE 10 for Windows 8. Move the cursor over the bottom right-hand corner (or swipe from the side of the screen) and click or tap on the **Settings Charm**

Don't forget

Some tasks within IE 10 require add-on apps to perform them. When one of these tasks is undertaken, you will be prompted to download the relevant add-on.

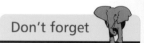

2 Click or tap on the **Internet Options** link

Don't forget

One of the Options is to turn on the Flip ahead function (see page 179).

3 Options can be applied for deleting the browsing history, whether websites have to ask permission if they are trying to use your physical location, the zoom settings for sites, turning On the Flip ahead functionality and encoding options if a page is not displaying correctly

Sharing in IE 10

When it comes to sharing web pages with other people the functionality of the Windows 8 interface really comes into its own. This is one area where the Charms can be used to connect and utilize other apps. To do this:

1 Open the web page that you want to share and access the **Share Charm**

2 The Share options include emailing specific contacts directly, or opening the Mail and People apps to select people for sharing with

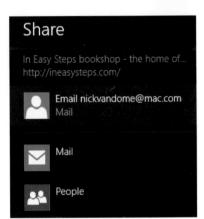

Don't forget

If you choose to share via the Mail or People apps, you have to select a contact and the web page will then be emailed to them.

3 For the direct email option, an email is created with the selected recipient. The email contains a link to the web page and a brief description of it

Printing in IE 10

The Charms can also be used to print active web pages.

 Open the web page that you want to print and access the **Devices Charm**

Devices

Click or tap on the device you want to use

Devices

Internet Explorer

Dell Laser Printer 1720dn (Cop...
Offline

Adobe PDF

Send To OneNote 2010

Microsoft XPS Document Writer

Don't forget

Many websites have a print version that is optimized for the printing process.

The web page is displayed in Print Preview

Select the number of prints and the orientation (Portrait or Landscape). Click or tap on the **More settings** link for additional print options

Copies

1   + −

Orientation

Portrait

More settings

Click or tap on the **Print** button

Print

Searching in IE 10

Searching for content is an integral part of using the web. This can be done with a search engine on the web itself, or the Search Charm can also be used within IE 10 in Windows 8 mode.

1   Open IE 10 in Windows 8 mode and click or tap on the **Search Charm**

2   Make sure that Internet Explorer is the option selected to search over

3   Enter a search word or phrase. Click or tap on the magnifier button to search over the keyword, or click or tap on one of the suggestions below the search box

Search

Internet Explorer

vandome   ✕   🔍

vandome

vandome

vandome **gallery**

vendome **pictures**

vandome **night club new haven may 2...**

vandome **movie list**

4   The search results are displayed within the search window. Click or tap on one of the links to go to that page

Flip Ahead in IE 10

The Flip ahead function in IE 10 is one that facilitates the quick navigation between long pages of content that are linked together but appear as separate web pages. For instance, long documents that are traditionally linked with 'Read more' or 'Next page' links can now be viewed with Flip ahead. Results for web searches are another good option for this as it enables you to move quickly through multiple pages of results. To do this:

1 Access a web page with multiple linked pages, such as a search results page

2 Move the cursor over the middle-right edge and click or tap on this button

3 The next linked page is accessed without the need to activate another link

IE 10 on the Desktop

IE 10 for the Desktop will have a more familiar look and feel to users of previous versions of IE and it also has a wider range of functionality. It can be accessed in a couple of main ways:

1. Access the Internet Explorer icon on the Taskbar

2. Within IE 10 in Windows 8 mode, click or tap on the **Page Tools** button and click or tap on the **View on the desktop** link

The Desktop version of IE 10 includes:

Menu bar   Address bar (with URL)   Favorites bar   Tabbed browsing (multipage)

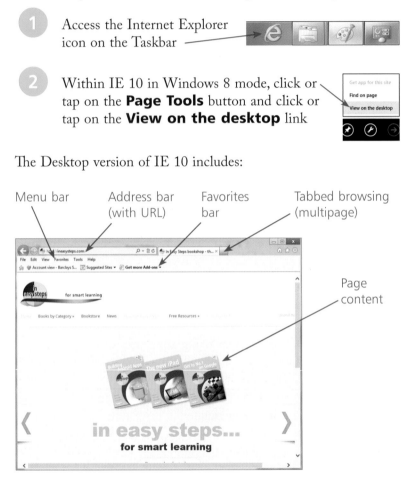

Page content

Menu Bar

At the top of the browser window is the Menu bar that contains sections with much of the functionality of IE 10. Click or tap on one of the headings to view the additional options. If there is an arrow next to an item it means that there are more options for this item.

View	Favorites	Tools	Help
Toolbars			▶
Quick tabs			Ctrl+Q
Explorer bars			▶
Go to			▶
Stop			Esc
Refresh			F5
Zoom (100%)			▶

Browser Controls

The Desktop version of IE 10 has considerable functionality:

Back and Forward

Select the **back** and **forward** buttons
to switch between recently-visited web
pages, or hold on one of the buttons to
select an entry from the Recent Pages list.

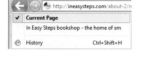

Tabs

Tabs allow you to view multiple web pages in
the same Internet Explorer window (see
page 186).

The Address Bar

This is where web addresses are
entered and includes access to
the Search box, a page compatibility view and the **Refresh** and
Stop buttons to control the loading of the web page specified in
the address box. This changes to the **Go To** button when a web
address is entered.

The Search Box

The Address Bar can also be used as a
Search Box. To do this, enter a word
in the Address Bar. In the results
window, click or tap on **Turn On
Suggestions**. The results will be
displayed as links to web pages and
search suggestions.

Command Bar

This is accessed from
the **View > Toolbars**
option on the Menu bar and contains items for setting the Home
page, RSS feeds, reading emails, printing, page information and
safety items such as deleting browsing history and selecting
InPrivate Browsing, and web page tools.

Favorites Button and Favorites Center

The Favorites button displays the Favorites
Center, with the favorites, feeds and website
history (see page 182).

Don't forget

InPrivate Browsing is
a way of viewing web
pages without any of the
information being stored
by the browser. For
instance, it will not show
up in your browsing
history or store cookies.

Bookmark Favorites

If you see a web page that you want to revisit, add it to your Favorites list to save having to record or remember the address.

Hot tip

Open the Favorites Center as shown on the previous page and click on this button to pin it within the browser window so that it stays open.

1 While viewing the page, click or tap on the **Favorites** button (see page 181) and then click or tap on the **Add to Favorites** button (or press **Ctrl** + **D**)

Add to favorites	▼	✕
	Add to favorites...	Ctrl+D

Add a Favorite ✕

☆ **Add a Favorite**
Add this webpage as a favorite. To access your favorites, visit the Favorites Center.

Name: PC Gaming - Microsoft Store Online

Create in: ☆ Favorites ▼   New folder

Add   Cancel

---

2 The page title is used as the name for the new favorite, but you can type an alternative name if you wish

3 Select **Add** to save the details in your Favorites list

View Favorites

1 Select the Favorites Center button and click or tap on the **Favorites** button (if not already selected)

Add to favorites	▼

Favorites	Feeds	History

📁 Favorites Bar

🔲 PC Gaming - Microsoft Store Online

2 Click or tap on a folder name to expand it

3 Click or tap any Favorites entry to display that web page

Hot tip

You can also right-click any link in a web page or in search results, and select **Add to favorites**.

4 Click or tap on **Add to favorites** and **Organize favorites**, to move, rename or delete the entries

Add to favorites	▼	✕
	Add to favorites...	Ctrl+D
	Add to Favorites bar	
	Add current tabs to favorites...	
	Import and export...	
	Organize favorites...	

RSS Feeds

RSS (Really Simple Syndication) Feeds provide the frequently-updated content from a news or blog website. Internet Explorer can discover and display feeds as you visit websites, or you can subscribe to feeds to automatically check for and download updates that you can view later.

Discover a Feed

1 Open Internet Explorer and browse to a website that has feeds, for example the CNN website (www.cnn.com). The Feeds button changes color to let you know

2 Click or tap on the arrow next to the **Feeds** button to see the list of feeds available

No Web Slices Found

CNN - Top Stories [RSS] (new)

3 Click or tap on one of the feeds to view the contents and you are offered the opportunity to subscribe, so that feed updates will be automatically downloaded

4 Select **Subscribe to this feed**, then click or tap the **Subscribe** button, to add the feed to your list in the Favorites Center

Don't forget

To view your subscribed feeds, select the **Favorites Center** button and then select the **Feeds** button.

Add to Favorites bar

Favorites	Feeds	History

CNN.com - Top Stories

183

History

1   Open the Favorites Center and select the **History** tab

Add to favorites ▼
Favorites   Feeds   **History**
View By Date
🔲 Monday
🔲 Tuesday
🔲 Wednesday
🔲 Today
az307127.vo.msecnd (az307127.vo...
bbc (www.bbc.co.uk)
bing (www.bing.com)
facebook (www.facebook.com)
google (www.google.co.uk)
Google
hs.windows.microsoft (hs.window...
iegallery (www.iegallery.com)
ineasysteps (ineasysteps.com)
About In Easy Steps | In Easy St...
Browse our Bookstore | In Easy...
Business and Professional Skill...
In Easy Steps bookshop - the h...
News | In Easy Steps

2   Pin the Favorites Center to the window (see page 182), so you can browse the History entries

3   Select the **down arrow** on the bar below the History tab, to change the sort order for the entries

Favorites   Feeds   **History**
View By Date ✔
View By Date
View By Site
View By Most Visited
View By Order Visited Today
Search History

Manage the History

1   From the Menu bar select **Tools > Internet options** and select the **General** tab

Browsing history
Delete temporary files, history, cookies, saved passwords, and web form information.
☐ Delete browsing history on exit
     [Delete...]   [Settings]

2   At Browsing history, select **Delete** to remove the records, or **Settings** to change the history period (default 20 days)

Home Page

Your home page is displayed when you start Internet Explorer or when you click the Home button. The web page displayed may be the Windows default, or may have been defined by your ISP or your computer supplier. However, you can choose any web page as your home page.

Current Web Page

1. With the preferred web page displayed, select the arrow next to the **Home** button on the Command bar and select **Add or change home page**

2. Select **Use this webpage as your only home page** or select another option

Reset Home Page

1. Select **Tools > Internet Options** and select the **General** tab

2. Select **Use default** to use the default home page specified by Internet Explorer

   or

   Select **Use new tab** to specify a home page for when a new tab is created

3. Click or tap **OK** to save the changes

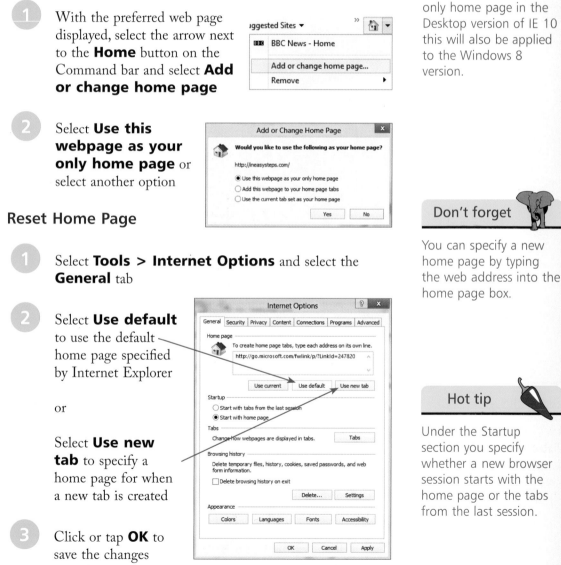

Hot tip

If a page is set as your only home page in the Desktop version of IE 10 this will also be applied to the Windows 8 version.

Don't forget

You can specify a new home page by typing the web address into the home page box.

Hot tip

Under the Startup section you specify whether a new browser session starts with the home page or the tabs from the last session.

Tabbed Browsing

You can open multiple websites in a single browser window, with each web page on a separate tab.

Don't forget

To open a web page link in a new tab, press **Ctrl** as you click or right-click the link (or press and hold on the link) and select **Open in new tab**.

Hot tip

Right-click on a tab at the top of the browser window for a menu of options relating to the tab, even if it is not currently active.

Hot tip

To save the group of tabs for reuse at any time, click or tap on **Add to favorites** (see page 182) and select Add current tabs to favorites.

 1 To open another tab, click or tap on the **New Tab** button

2 Type an address in the Address Bar and press **Enter** or click or tap on one of the frequently-visited sites

3 To switch between tabs, select the page tab on the tab row

4 Close IE 10 and you will be asked if you want to **Close all tabs** or just **Close current tab**

5 You can Reopen closed tabs from a new tab by clicking or tapping on the **Reopen closed tabs** link and selecting the tab, or tabs, that you want to reopen

Zoom

Internet Explorer Zoom allows you to enlarge or reduce your view of a web page; it enlarges everything on the web page (image and text).

1 Select **View > Zoom** from the Menu bar to select options for viewing a web page

2 Select to zoom in or out or select an option for one of the predefined zoom levels (for example, 400%)

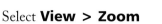

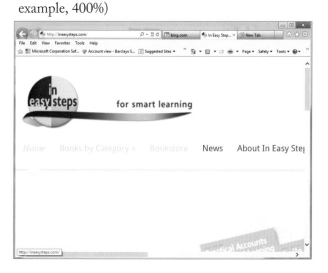

Hot tip

Reduce (zoom out) to get an overall view of a large web page. Enlarge (zoom in) to see the fine detail for one section of the page.

Don't forget

Select Custom to specify a magnification factor from 10% to 1000%.

Wheel Mouse Zoom

1 If you have a wheel mouse, hold down **Ctrl** and scroll the wheel to zoom in or out

Keyboard Zoom

1 Press **Ctrl −** to reduce, or **Ctrl +** to enlarge, in 25% increments. Press **Ctrl + *** to return to 100%

Print

In IE 10 on the Desktop, it is possible to print directly from the Command bar. To do this:

Don't forget

The print is automatically scaled to fit the paper size so that you will not find the right-hand edge chopped off.

1 Select the **Print** button on the Command bar, and Internet Explorer automatically prints the current tab

Use Print Preview to see how the printed web page will appear.

1 With the required web page open, click the arrow next to the print button and select **Print Preview**

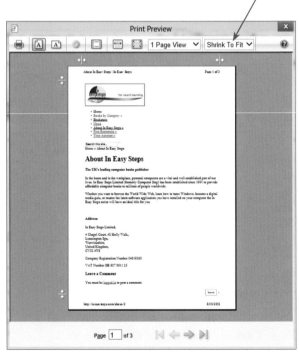

Hot tip

Select the **Portrait** or **Landscape** buttons to quickly reorientate the print image.

2 Note that the Shrink to Fit option is preselected in the Change Print Size box

188

Don't forget

You can select a print zoom factor from 30% to 200%, or enter a custom value. Full page view also offers easy-to-adjust margin handles.

3 To illustrate the benefit of this, click the **down arrow** and select 100% and see how the print width changes

10 Keeping in Touch

There are several Windows 8 apps for keeping in touch with people. This chapter details how to use the Mail, People, Messaging and Calendar apps.

Setting Up Mail

Email has become an essential part of everyday life, both socially and in the business world. Windows 8 accommodates this with the Mail app. This can be used to link to online services such as GMail and Outlook (the renamed version of Hotmail) and also other email accounts. To set up an email account with Mail:

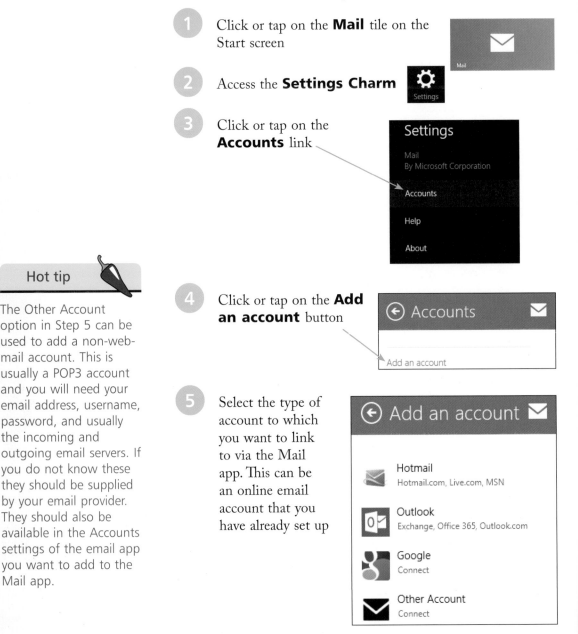

1. Click or tap on the **Mail** tile on the Start screen

2. Access the **Settings Charm**

3. Click or tap on the **Accounts** link

    Settings
    Mail
    By Microsoft Corporation

    Accounts

    Help

    About

Hot tip

The Other Account option in Step 5 can be used to add a non-webmail account. This is usually a POP3 account and you will need your email address, username, password, and usually the incoming and outgoing email servers. If you do not know these they should be supplied by your email provider. They should also be available in the Accounts settings of the email app you want to add to the Mail app.

4. Click or tap on the **Add an account** button

    ⬅ Accounts

    Add an account

5. Select the type of account to which you want to link to via the Mail app. This can be an online email account that you have already set up

    ⬅ Add an account

    Hotmail
    Hotmail.com, Live.com, MSN

    Outlook
    Exchange, Office 365, Outlook.com

    Google
    Connect

    Other Account
    Connect

6　Enter your current login details for the selected email account and click or tap on the **Connect** button

Add your Google account

Enter the information below to connect to your Google account.

Email address
nickvandome@googlemail.com

Password
••••••••

Connect　Cancel

191

7　Once it has been connected, the details of the account are shown under the Mail heading, including the mailboxes within the account. Click or tap on the Inbox to view the emails within it

Mail

Google　11

Inbox 11

Drafts

Sent items

Outbox

Junk

Deleted items

8　The list of emails appear in the left-hand pane Click or tap on a message to view it in the reading pane. Click or tap on this button to go back to the main window

Google Inbox

Today's Top 5 Investing Ideas
One of the Best Ways to Build a Dividend Portfolio I've Ever Seen
To: Nick Vandome

TODAY'S TOP 5 INVESTING IDEAS

Fill Up Your Car For $2.14 a Gallon
There is a trend popping up on the nation's highways of fueling stations offering transportation fuel at a 43% discount. And investors in the company making it possible stand to make a killing...

Is it Time for You to Finally Sell Coca-Cola?
Short sellers are flocking to this stock, which doesn't make sense, until you dig a little deeper.

One of the Best Ways to Build a Dividend Portfolio I've Ever Seen
This high-yielding investment is a great low-risk opportunity that rewards its investors with generous dividends.

The Surprising Place where the Wealthiest 6% Make Their Millions (sponsor)
Most people don't even realize this exists... but there's a private stock market where politicians, rock stars, and royalty have made their fortunes for years. And now, you can too. We'll show you how, here.

Working with Mail

Once you have set up an account in the Mail app you can then start creating and managing your emails with it.

 On the Inbox page, select an email and click or tap on this button to respond

<table>
<tr><td>**Reply**</td></tr>
<tr><td>**Reply all**</td></tr>
<tr><td>**Forward**</td></tr>
</table>

 Select an email and click or tap on this button to delete it

Composing email

To compose and send an email message:

1 Click or tap on this button to create a new message

 Click or tap in the To field and enter an email address

 Click or tap on the **More details** link to access options for blind copying and priority level

4 The email address can be in the format of myname@gmail.com or enter the name of one of your contacts in the People app and the email address will be entered automatically

5 Enter a subject heading and body text to the email

Good news!

Guess what, I won the competition. I've attached a picture!

Sent from Windows Mail

6 Access the toolbar as shown in Step 10 and click or tap on the **Attachments** button

7 Click or tap on a folder from which you want to attach the file

Files ˅ Pictures

Go up   Sort by name ˅

Nick

Scenery

Screenshots

8 Select a file and click or tap on the **Attach** button

nick6
7/4/2010 11:12 AM
58.9 KB

Attach

9 The file is shown in the body of the email

Good news!

1 file attached   Send using SkyDrive instead

Guess what, I won the competition. I've attached a picture!

Sent from Windows Mail

Don't forget

The bottom toolbar can also be accessed by pressing **WinKey + Z**.

10 Select an item of text or right-click or swipe up from the bottom of the screen to access the text formatting options

Save draft   Attachments   Paste   Font   Bold   Italic   Underline   Text colour   Emoticons   More

Hot tip

Emoticons (or smileys) can be accessed from the bottom toolbar, for insertion into emails.

11 Click or tap on this button to send the email

Sharing with Mail

It is great to share items via email, whether it is photos, music or video clips. There is no share function directly from Mail (although items can be added with the Attachments option) but items can be shared directly via email through their own apps and the Share Charm. To do this:

 Open an item you want to share, such an image in the Photos app

 Access the **Share Charm**

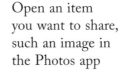

Select the **Mail** app as the method for sharing the item

Share

1 photo
File from the Photos app

 Mail

The photo is attached to an email in the Mail app. Enter a recipient and subject and send as with a regular email

Searching within Mail

As you get more and more emails it may become difficult to find items within specific messages. To help find things, the Search Charm can be made to search text in email subject headings and body text.

1 Open Mail and access the **Search Charm**

Search

2 Make sure that the **Mail** option is selected as the item to search over

Mail

3 Enter a word or phrase into the Search box and click or tap on this icon to perform the search

Search

Mail

income   ✕ 🔍

4 The results are displayed underneath the Inbox heading. Click or tap on an item to open the related email

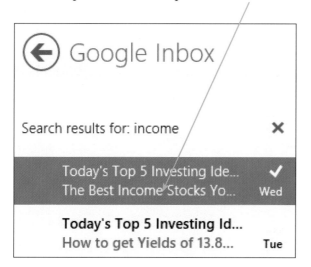

← Google Inbox

Search results for: income   ✕

Today's Top 5 Investing Ide...   ✓
The Best Income Stocks Yo...   Wed

Today's Top 5 Investing Id...
How to get Yields of 13.8...   Tue

Don't forget

The Search Charm works over all mailboxes and all of the content in emails, not just the subject title.

Hot tip

You can move an email to different mailboxes by selecting it and then accessing the bottom toolbar. Click or tap on the **Move** button and navigate to the mailbox that you want to use.

195

Finding People

An electronic address book is always a good feature to have on a computer and with Windows 8 this function is provided by the People app. This not only allows you to add your own contacts manually, you can also link to any of your online services, such as Facebook, Twitter and LinkedIn and import the contacts that you have here. To do this:

 Click or tap on the **People** tile on the Start screen

2 Click on the **Settings Charm** and click or tap on the **Accounts** link

Settings

People
By Microsoft Corporation

Accounts

Hot tip

You can also select accounts to add to the People app from the home page when you first open it.

3 The current accounts linked to the People app are listed. Click or tap on the **Add an account** link

Don't forget

If your contacts are using Windows 8 you will be able to notify them of any updates through Facebook, Twitter or LinkedIn as long as they have these services added in their People app, and you are one of their contacts.

4 Select the account or service from which you would like to import your contacts

5 When you connect to the selected service you will be asked to grant Microsoft access to this account. Enter your details (for the account you are linking to) and click or tap on the **Ok, I'll Allow It** button

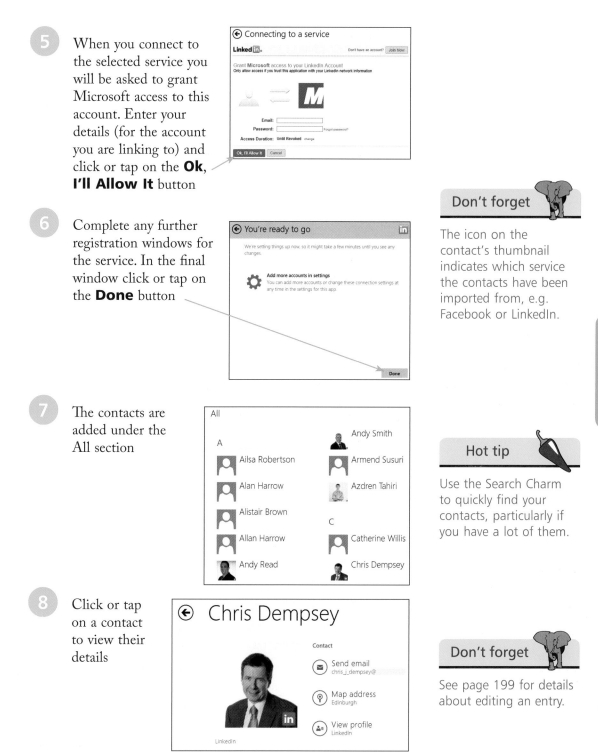

6 Complete any further registration windows for the service. In the final window click or tap on the **Done** button

The icon on the contact's thumbnail indicates which service the contacts have been imported from, e.g. Facebook or LinkedIn.

7 The contacts are added under the All section

Hot tip

Use the Search Charm to quickly find your contacts, particularly if you have a lot of them.

8 Click or tap on a contact to view their details

Don't forget

See page 199 for details about editing an entry.

...cont'd

Adding contacts manually

As well as importing contacts, it is also possible to enter them manually into the People app:

1 Right-click in the People window, or swipe up from the bottom of the window and click or tap on the **New** button

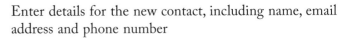

2 Enter details for the new contact, including name, email address and phone number

To delete a contact, click or tap on them to view their details. Then access the bottom toolbar and click or tap on the **Delete** button to remove them.

New contact

Account		Name	Address
Microsoft		Email	Address
Name		Personal	Other info
First name		lucyvandome@gmail.com	Other info
Lucy		Email	
Last name		Phone	
Vandome		Mobile	
Company		07777123456	
		Phone	

Save   Cancel

3 Click or tap on the plus sign next to a field to access additional options for that item

(+) Name

- Phonetic first name
- Middle name
- Phonetic last name
- Phonetic company
- Nickname
- Title
- Suffix

4 Click or tap on the **Save** button to create the new contact

Save

5 Click or tap on a contact in the People window to view their details

6 To edit a contact's details, right-click or swipe up from the bottom of the window and click or tap on the **Edit** button. This brings up the same window in Step 2, on the previous page, where the details can be edited

7 Click or tap on the **What's new** link to view any updates or notifications

What's new
See friends' posts and more

from your contacts. This could include Facebook, Twitter and LinkedIn updates

8 Click or tap on the **Me** link to view your profile. If you have a Microsoft Account the details will come from this

Social

Me

9 Right-click or swipe up from the bottom of the window and click or tap on the **Edit** button to edit your own profile

Chatting with Messaging

As long as you have a Microsoft Account, you can use the Messaging app to have text chats with other users of Messaging and also other compatible messaging services. You can also connect to other services and add your contacts for messaging.

1 Click or tap on the Messaging tile on the Start screen

2 Access the **Settings Charm** and click or tap on the **Accounts** link

3 Click or tap on the **Add an account** link, or

4 On the Messaging home screen, click or tap on one of the items to add to your account

5 Complete the registration screens to connect to the selected service and add your contacts so that you can message them when they are online

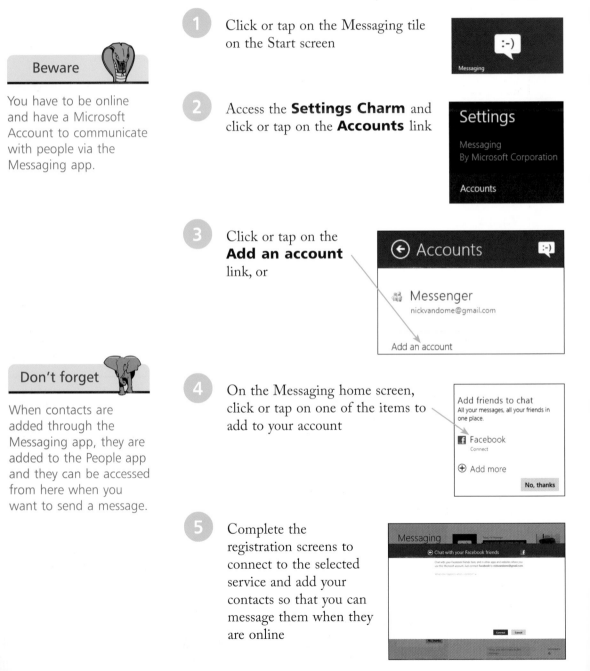

Starting to message

You can send messages to other people if they are online and using a compatible messaging service.

1 The current conversations are listed in the left-hand pane

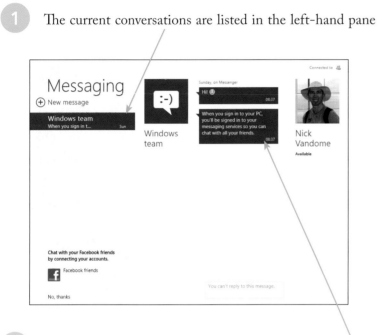

2 The items in a conversation thread are shown in the main window area

3 Right-click or swipe up from the bottom of the screen to access the toolbar and click or tap on the **New message** button to create a new conversation

4 The New option opens up the People app from where you can select from all of your contacts or only those currently online

5 On the toolbar, click or tap on the **Status** button to select your status as it will appear for other people when you are messaging them, or they are looking to invite you to a new conversation

Don't forget

To delete a conversation thread, right-click on the window, or swipe up from the bottom of the screen and click or tap on the **Delete** button.

Don't forget

You can also invite other people to chat, through the Messenger section of the online Profile Live website. To do this, access the bottom toolbar and click or tap on the **Invite** button and click or tap on the **Add a new friend** link. On the Profile Live page, enter the email address of the person you want to invite.

201

Using the Calendar

The Calendar app can be used to include important events and reminders. To view the calendar:

1 Click or tap on the **Calendar** tile on the Start screen

2 The calendar is displayed by default in month view, with some important events and holidays already included. Click or tap on an item to view its details

3 Click, tap or swipe here to move backwards or forwards through the calendar

4 Right-click or swipe up from the bottom of the screen to access the Calendar toolbar. Click or tap on this button to view the current day

5 Click or tap on these buttons to view different formats for the calendar

Adding events

Events can be added to the calendar and various settings can be applied to them such as recurrence and reminders.

1 Click or tap on a date or right-click or swipe up from the bottom of the screen and click or tap on the **New** button to create a new event

2 Enter details for the event including the location, the time and the duration. Enter a title for the event here and any message you want to add to it

Details   Dad's birthday   🗑 💾 ✕

When
25 Sunday ▾   November ▾   2012 ▾   Come and join us!

Start
12 ▾   30 ▾

How long
2 hours ▾

Where
Home

Calendar
■ Nick's calendar—nickvandome@gmail.com

How often
Once ▾

Reminder
15 minutes ▾

Status
Busy ▾

☐ Private

203

3 Click or tap on the **Start** field and enter a time for the event. Set its duration in the **How long** field

Start
12 ▾   30 ▾
How long
2 hours ▾

4 If **All day** is selected in the **How long** field the time in the **Start** field will be grayed-out

Start
0 ▾   00 ▾
How long
All day ▾

...cont'd

5 For a recurring event, click or tap in the **How often** box

How often

Once

6 Select an option for the recurrence, such as **Every year** for a birthday

Once

Every day

Every weekday

Every week

Every month

Every year

7 Click or tap on the **Save** button to save the event, or click or tap on the cross button to delete it

8 To delete an existing event, click or tap on it to open it

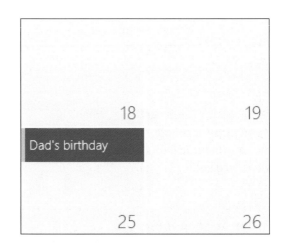

18   19

Dad's birthday

25   26

9 Right-click or swipe up from the bottom of the screen and click or tap on the **Delete** button

Delete

11 Networking

There is a built-in networking capability within Windows 8, allowing you to share a variety of items between two or more computers. This chapter shows how this can be done and how to set up the invaluable HomeGroup feature for file sharing.

Network Components

There are numerous possibilities for setting up a home network. To start with, there are two major network technologies:

- Wired – e.g. Ethernet, using twisted pair cables, to send data at rates of 10, 100 or 1000 Mbps (megabits per second)

- Wireless – using radio waves to send data at rates of 11 or 54 Mbps (or up to, in theory, 300 Mbps with the latest devices)

There is also a variety of hardware items needed:

- Network adapter – appropriate to the network type, with one for each computer in the network

- Network controller – one or more hub, switch or router, providing the actual connection to each network adapter

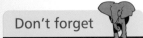

Don't forget

The network adapter can be connected to the USB port, inserted in the PC Card slot or installed inside your computer.

Don't forget

Ethernet adapters connect to a network hub, switch or wired router. Wireless adapters connect through a wireless router or a combination of router/switch.

Hot tip

You may already have some of these elements in operation, if you have an existing network running a previous version of Windows.

Internet   Modem
Ethernet Adapters
Router
Wireless Adapters

There is also the Internet connection (dial-up, DSL or cable) using:

- A modem connected to one of the computers

- A modem connected to the network

- Internet access incorporated into the router or switch

Set Up Your Network

The steps you will need, and the most appropriate sequence to follow, will depend on the specific options on your system. However, the main steps will include:

- Install network adapters in the computers, where necessary
- Set up or verify the Internet connection
- Configure the wireless router or access point
- Connect other computers and start up Windows on each PC

Install Hardware

If you need to install a wired or wireless network adapter, follow the instructions provided with the adapter. For example, to install the Linksys Wireless-N USB adapter:

 Insert the CD provided and the setup program will start up automatically. Select the **Click Here to Start** button

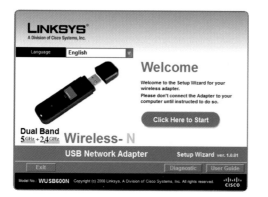

Follow the instructions (giving permission for access where requested) to complete the software installation

When prompted, attach the adapter to a USB port, via a cable if needed

When Windows has detected the wireless networks in your neighborhood, select your network and click or tap on the **Connect** button

Hot tip

With all the options and combinations that might be available, configuring the network could be complex. However, Windows 8 is designed to automate as much of the task as possible.

Don't forget

Depending on the AutoPlay settings, you may be prompted to run the installation option when you insert the CD.

Beware

Enter the security key for your wireless network when prompted.

Internet Connection

You do not actually require an Internet connection to set up a network, if all you want to do is share files and printers. However, in most cases the main purpose of the network is to share your connection to the Internet across several computers.

Verify your Connection

If you already have an Internet connection, open your web browser and go to a website that gets regularly updated (e.g. a news site). If the website opens with up-to-date entries and you don't get any error messages your connection is working.

Install Router

You can use a router with a DSL modem (an Internet gateway) to make an Internet connection available for sharing. This is usually set up on one computer, connected via an Ethernet cable or a USB cable. A configuration program may be provided on an installation CD or you can use your web browser.

1　Open the browser and enter the IP address provided for the router, e.g. 192.168.1.254 or a similar local IP address

2　Select Settings and enter the administrator user name (if required) and password, as provided by your ISP

You will be using the default ID and password for the particular equipment. While this can only be accessed from a direct local connection, you may feel more secure if you change the password.

3. Select **Admin Password**, then enter the old password and the new password and click to **Change password**

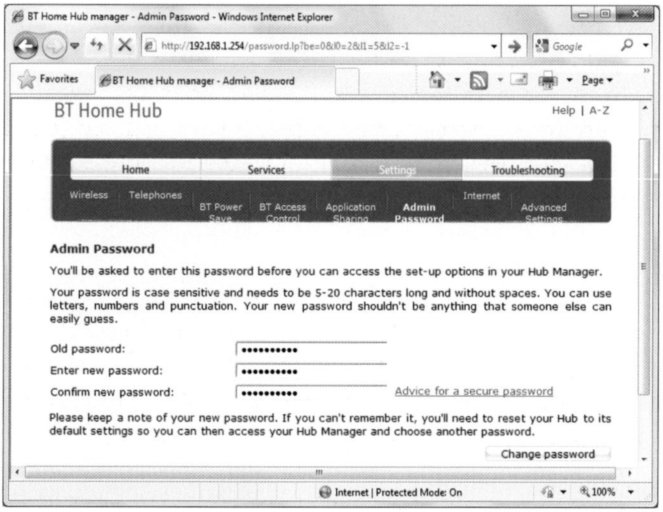

4. Select **Wireless** to change the setup, for example by providing a new SSID (Service Set Identifier, the wireless network name) and choosing the encryption type and key

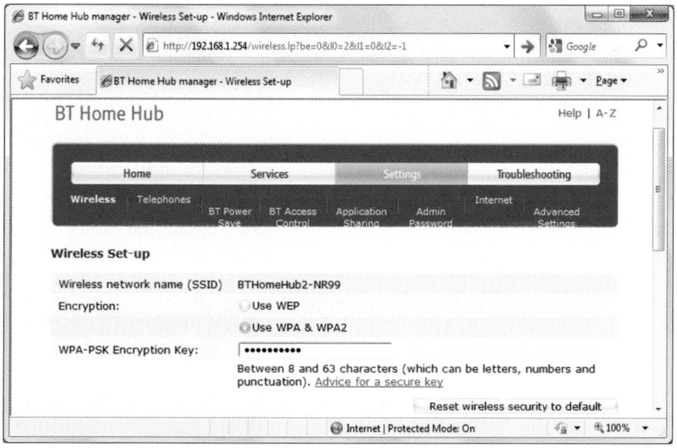

5. You can also change the channels used for the wireless communications, if you have problems with network range or speed, or interference from other devices

Don't forget

The options offered will depend on the particular features of your router or gateway device, but they should, in principle, be similar.

Beware

Do not use the default values for the parameters since these could be known to other people.

Discover Networks

Connect your computers to form your network, using Ethernet cables and adapters or by setting up your wireless adapters and routers. When you start up each computer, Windows 8 will examine the current configuration and discover any new networks that have been established since the last start up. You can check this, or connect manually to a network, from within the default settings from the Settings Charm. To do this:

1 Click or tap on the **Settings Charm** and click or tap on the **Network** button

2 Under the Wi-Fi heading, click or tap on one of the available networks

3 Check on the **Connect automatically** box and click or tap on the **Connect** button to connect to the selected network

4 The selected network is shown as Connected. This is also shown on the Settings Charm in Step 1

Network and Sharing Center

The Network and Sharing Center within the Control Panel is where you can view settings for your network.

① To open the Network and Sharing Center, access the Control Panel and click or tap on the **Network and Internet** link

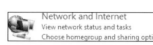

② Click or tap on the **Network and Sharing Center** link

③ Details of the current network are displayed in the Network and Sharing Center

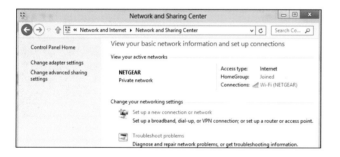

④ Click or tap on the **Connections** link to see details of your Wi-Fi connection

⑤ The Wi-Fi information is displayed. Click or tap on the **Properties** button for more information

Don't forget

The Network and Sharing Center displays network settings and provides access to networking tasks for the computer.

Hot tip

In the Network and Sharing Center, click or tap on the **Set up a new connection or network** link to create a different network from the one currently in use.

Join the HomeGroup

A HomeGroup is a network function that enables a
Windows 8 computer to connect to another Windows 8 machine
(or Windows 7) and share content. There are different ways to
join a HomeGroup, depending whether you connect from the
Windows 8 interface, or through the Control Panel.

Connecting through the Windows 8 interface

To connect to a HomeGroup from the Windows 8 interface:

Don't forget

When you add a
computer to your
network, Windows 8
on that computer will
detect that there is a
HomeGroup already
created.

212

Don't forget

Only computers on the
same Home network and
running the Windows 7
or 8 operating system
(any edition) will be
invited to join the
HomeGroup.

1 Access the **Settings Charm** and click
or tap on the **Change PC settings**
button

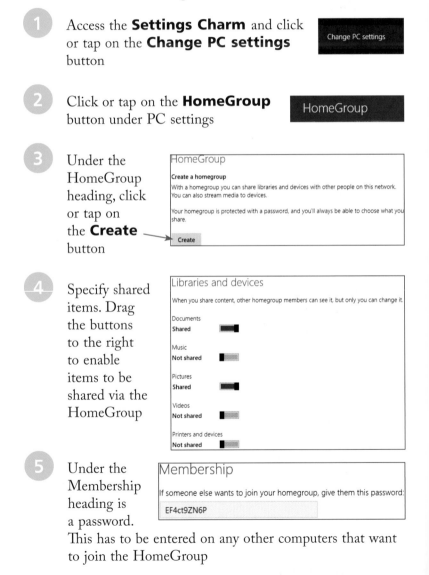

Change PC settings

2 Click or tap on the **HomeGroup**
button under PC settings

HomeGroup

3 Under the
HomeGroup
heading, click
or tap on
the **Create**
button

HomeGroup

Create a homegroup
With a homegroup you can share libraries and devices with other people on this network.
You can also stream media to devices.

Your homegroup is protected with a password, and you'll always be able to choose what you
share.

Create

4 Specify shared
items. Drag
the buttons
to the right
to enable
items to be
shared via the
HomeGroup

Libraries and devices

When you share content, other homegroup members can see it, but only you can change it.

Documents
Shared

Music
Not shared

Pictures
Shared

Videos
Not shared

Printers and devices
Not shared

5 Under the
Membership
heading is
a password.

Membership

If someone else wants to join your homegroup, give them this password:

EF4ct9ZN6P

This has to be entered on any other computers that want
to join the HomeGroup

Connecting through the Control Panel

To join a HomeGroup from the Control Panel

1 Access **Network and Internet** in the Control Panel and click or tap on the **HomeGroup** link

Beware

HomeGroup applies to any user with an account on the computer, so if a different user logs on, the associated files will also be accessible.

2 Click or tap on the **Next** button to start setting up the HomeGroup

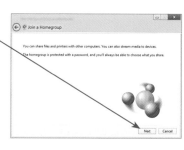

Don't forget

Windows generates the password when the HomeGroup is created (see page 212). If you forget the password, you can find it in the Control Panel on any computer already joined to the HomeGroup.

3 You can view details of the HomeGroup you want to join. Click or tap on the **Join now** button

213

4 Select the items that you want to share in the HomeGroup and click or tap on the **Next** button

5 Enter the password that has to be provided from the other computer

Hot tip

If there is a printer to be shared, Windows 8 will automatically take the action needed to make it available on the network.

6 Once you have joined the HomeGroup you will be able to share your files on the other computer and vice versa

Sharing Files and Folders

There are different ways in which you can share items once a HomeGroup has been set up:

1 Open the File Explorer and select the **HomeGroup** in the Library pane and click or tap on the **Share libraries** button in the Share section of the File Explorer

> **Don't forget**
>
> The Share section in File Explorer is accessed from the Scenic Ribbon.

2 Select the items that you want to share with the HomeGroup. This will be done automatically, i.e. if you share Pictures then all of the items in the Pictures library will be shared, as will new ones that are added

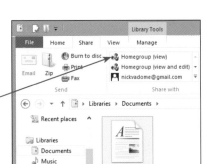

3 To share a specific item, select it in the File Explorer and click or tap on the **HomeGroup** button in the Share section

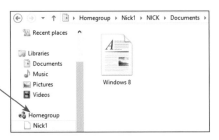

4 Select the HomeGroup in the Navigation pane of the File Explorer Library pane to view the shared item in Step 3

Sharing Settings

Within the Network and Sharing Center there are also options for specifying how items are shared over the network, not just in the HomeGroup. To select these:

1 Open the Network and Sharing Center and click or tap on the **Change advanced sharing settings** link

2 Select sharing options for different networks, including private, guest or public and all networks. Options can be selected for turning on network discovery so that your computer can see other computers on the network, and file and printer sharing

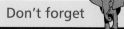

Don't forget

If you are sharing over a network you should be able to access the Public folder on another computer (providing that network discovery is turned on). If you are the administrator of the other computer you will also be able to access your own home folder, although you will need to enter the required password for this.

3 Click or tap on these buttons to view the options for each network category

Sharing a Printer

When you join a HomeGroup, Windows may detect a shared printer. However, the software drivers required may not be installed on this machine. To make the printer available

1 Click or tap on the **Install printer** button

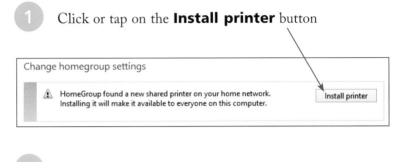

2 Click or tap on the **Install driver** button, to confirm you trust the computer and network sharing the printer

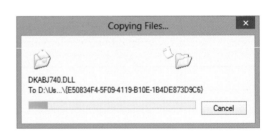

3 The driver files are copied to your computer

Beware

If you are using a shared printer, the computer from where you are sharing it has to be turned on in order for you to use the printer.

4 The shared printer is added to the Devices and Printers section in the Control Panel

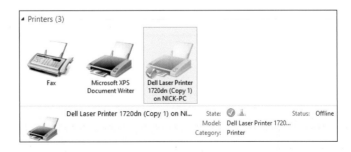

View Network Components

You can also view the network components in the network in File Explorer. To do this:

1 Open File Explorer and click or tap on the **Network** link

2 To view the shared items offered by a particular computer, for example the Nick-PC, double-click or tap on the associated icon

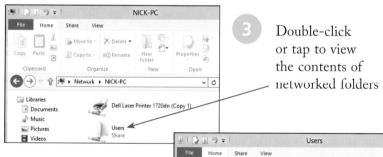

3 Double-click or tap to view the contents of networked folders

Public files and folders plus those belonging to the currently-active user are available for access. Items can be copied here for sharing purposes.

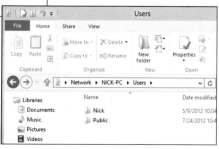

Don't forget

The Public folder on your own computer can be used to make items available to other users on the network.

Network Troubleshooting

1 Open the Network and Sharing Center and select **Troubleshoot problems**

> Troubleshoot problems
> Diagnose and repair network problems, or get troubleshooting information.

2 Windows searches online for troubleshooting packs

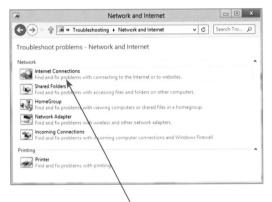

Windows 8 provides several troubleshooters to resolve common problems with networks. They are downloaded, so you always get the most up-to-date help.

218

3 Select, for example, Shared Folders and follow the prompts to describe and hopefully resolve the problems

Hot tip

In this case, a problem accessing a folder on another computer is quickly resolved as a typing error, when Windows says it cannot find "windows8" but detects the similar folder name "Windows 8" (with a space before 8).

12 System and Security

Windows 8 includes tools
to enhance the security,
performance and reliability
of your computer. It helps
you to maintain your hard
drive at peak efficiency,
protects your computer from
malicious software and
keeps your system up to date.

System Properties

There are several ways to open the System Properties, and view information about your computer:

1 Access the **Control Panel, System and Security** and then click or tap on the **System** category

2 Press the **WinKey** + the **Pause/Break** keys

3 Right-click **Computer** in the File Explorer and select **Properties** from the menu

4 Right-click in the bottom left-hand corner and select **System** from the contextual menu

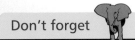

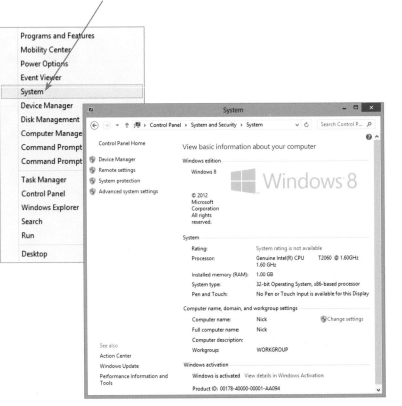

Device Manager

1. Select **Device Manager**, to list all of the hardware components that are installed on your computer

2. Select the ▷ symbol to expand that entry to show details

3. Select the ◢ symbol to collapse the expanded entry

4. Double-click or tap any device to open its properties

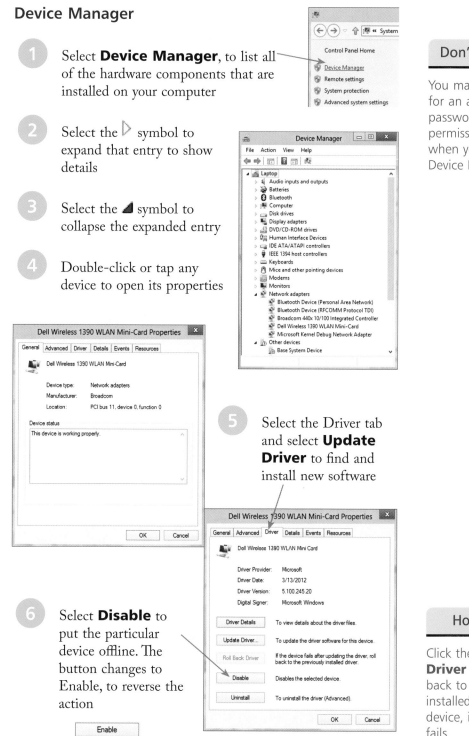

5. Select the Driver tab and select **Update Driver** to find and install new software

6. Select **Disable** to put the particular device offline. The button changes to Enable, to reverse the action

221

Performance Information

The System Properties panel displays the Windows Experience Index, the overall capability of your system. To view the details:

1 Open **System Properties** and click **Performance Information and Tools**

Performance Information and Tools

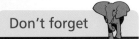

Don't forget

Processor, memory, graphics, gaming and hard disk facilities are assessed. Your Windows Experience rating (your base score) is determined by the lowest of these individual scores.

2 Click or tap on the **Rate this computer** button

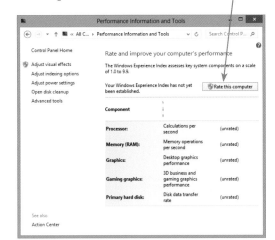

Hot tip

Click or tap on the **Advanced Tools** link to monitor the actual performance on your computer.

3 The results for your system are displayed:

4 If you upgrade any of the hardware components on your computer click or tap on the **Re-run the assessment** link to see the effect

Clean Up Your Disk

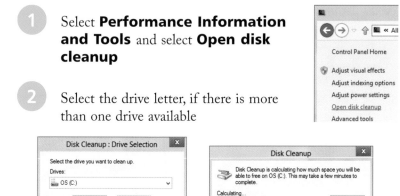

1. Select **Performance Information and Tools** and select **Open disk cleanup**

2. Select the drive letter, if there is more than one drive available

3. Disk Cleanup scans the drive to identify files that can be safely removed

4. All of the possible files are listed by category, and the sets of files recommended to be deleted are marked with a tick symbol

5. Make changes to the selections, clicking **View Files** if necessary to help you choose

6. Select the button **Clean up system files**, to include these also, then select **OK**

7. Deleted files will not be transferred to the Recycle Bin, so confirm that you do want to permanently delete all of these files. The files will be removed and the disk space will become available

Don't forget

You can have more than one hard disk on your computer, or you can divide one hard disk into several partitions, with separate drive letters.

223

...cont'd

When a file is written to the hard disk, it may be stored in several pieces in different places. This fragmentation of disk space can slow down your computer. Disk Defragmenter rearranges the data so the disk will work more efficiently.

1 In the File Manager, right-click on **OS (C:)** and click or tap on the **Properties** link

2 Select the **Tools** tab and click or tap on the **Optimize** button

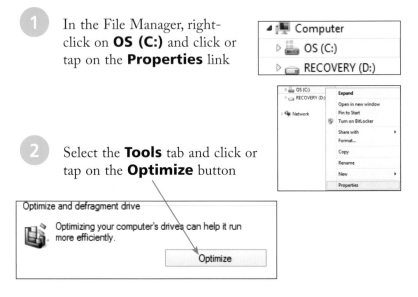

Optimize and defragment drive

 Optimizing your computer's drives can help it run more efficiently.

Optimize

3 The process runs as a scheduled task, but you can select a drive and select **Analyze disk** to check out a new drive

4 Click **Defragment disk** to process the selected disk. This may take from several minutes to several hours to complete, depending on the size and state of the disk, but you can still use your computer while the task is running

Back Up and Recover Data

1 Open **Control Panel** and select **Save backup copies of your files with File History**, in the System and Security category

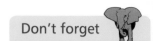

System and Security
Review your computer's status
Save backup copies of your files with File History
Find and fix problems

Don't forget

To make sure you do not lose the files stored on your computer, you should back them up regularly. Windows will help you set up automatic backups.

2 The first time you do this, you can select a drive such as an external hard drive or a network drive. Click or tap on the **Turn on** button to back up copies of your files

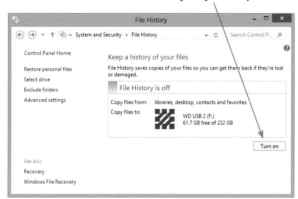

3 Details of the backup are displayed here

225

Hot tip

You can create a system image and also back up data files in the libraries and other folders on your system.

4 Click or tap on the **Run now** link to perform another backup

WD USB 2 (F:)
61.7 GB free of 232 GB

Files last copied on 07/09/2012 10:30.
Run now

System Restore

Windows 8 takes snapshots of the system files before any software updates are applied, or in any event once every seven days. You can also create a snapshot manually. The snapshots are known as Restore Points and are managed by System Restore.

1. Open **System Properties** (see page 220) and select **System protection**

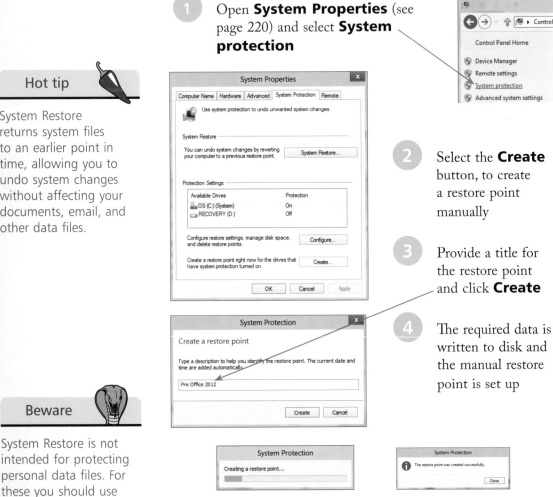

2. Select the **Create** button, to create a restore point manually

3. Provide a title for the restore point and click **Create**

4. The required data is written to disk and the manual restore point is set up

226

Using Restore Points

The installation of a new app or driver software may make Windows 8 behave unpredictably or have other unexpected results. Usually, uninstalling the app or rolling back the driver will correct the situation. If this does not fix the problem, use an automatic or manual restore point to reset your system to an earlier date when everything worked correctly.

System Restore...

1. Select **System Protection** and click the **System Restore** button

System Restore

Restore system files and settings

System Restore can help fix problems that might be making your computer run slowly or stop responding.

System Restore does not affect any of your documents, pictures, or other personal data. Recently installed programs and drivers might be uninstalled.

< Back   Next >   Cancel

2. By default this will offer to undo the most recent change. This may fix the problem

System Restore

Restore your computer to the state it was in before the selected event

Current time zone: GMT Daylight Time

Date and Time	Description	Type
6/11/2012 10:51:48 AM	Pre Office 2012	Manual
6/6/2012 11:30:39 AM	Windows Update	Critical Update

Scan for affected programs

< Back   Next >   Cancel

3. Otherwise, click **Choose a different restore point**, and pick a suitable time

4. Follow the prompts to restart the system using system files from the selected date and time

227

Action Center

The Action Center monitors security and system maintenance issues and delivers alerts for features such as Windows Backup.

1 Move the mouse over the Action Center icon on the Notifications section of the Taskbar to see the status. If a problem is detected, the icon is marked with a white cross in a red circle

2 Click or tap on the icon for more details, then select **Open Action Center**

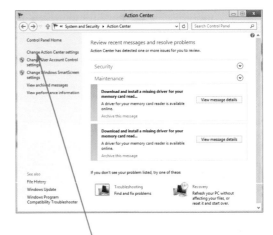

228

Hot tip

In the Action Center you can also change User Account Control settings and Windows Updates.

3 You can solve the problems from the Action Center, or click Change Action Center settings to adjust the alerts

Windows Firewall

1 Open Control Panel, select the System and Security category and select **Windows Firewall**

2 Select **Turn Windows Firewall on or off** to customize settings for private (home and work) and public networks

3 Select **Allow an app or feature through Windows Firewall**, to view the allowed apps

Allow an app or feature through Windows Firewall

4 Select **Allow another app**, if you need to Add an app

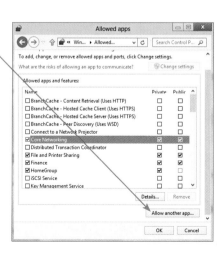

Hot tip

The Windows Firewall can be used to provide a level of protection against malicious software and viruses.

Don't forget

Firewall is on by default in Windows 8, but you can turn it off if you have another Firewall installed and active. Note that if you have a router with a built-in firewall, you still need the Windows 8 Firewall (or other firewall) on your computer.

Beware

Only add apps to the allowed list if you are advised to do so by a trusted advisor.

Malware Protection

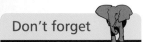
1 Open Control Panel, type *Defender* in the Search box and select **Windows Defender**

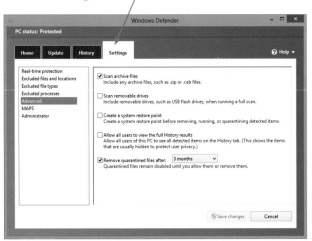

2 Click or tap on the **Settings** tab and adjust settings such as real-time protection, exclusions and advanced settings

3 For an immediate check, select the **Home** tab and click or tap on the **Scan now** button

Scan now

Windows Defender is scanning your PC

This might take some time, depending on the type of scan selected.

Cancel scan

Windows Update

Windows Update manages updates to Windows 8 and other Microsoft products. Applying updates can prevent or fix problems, improve the security or enhance performance, so Windows Update can be set up to install important updates automatically. To review your settings for Windows Update:

1 Select **Control Panel**, **System and Security** and select **Windows Update**

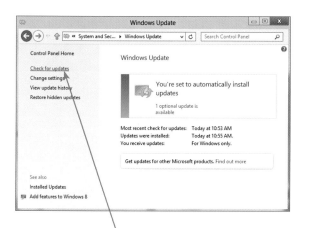

2 To see if there are any updates that are waiting to be downloaded and applied, select **Check for updates**

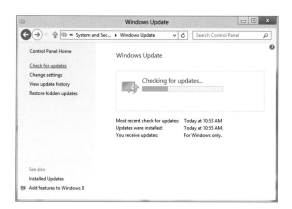

3 If there are updates, click or tap on **Install updates** to download and apply them immediately, or wait for Windows Update to install them at the scheduled time

Hot tip

Alternatively, you can click **Windows Update** from Action Center.

Don't forget

Click or tap on **View update history** to see the changes that have previously been applied to your system.

Don't forget

See page 232 for details about changing the settings for how Windows Update functions.

Change Settings

① Open Windows Update and select **Change settings**

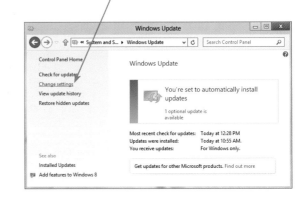

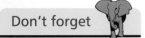
② The recommended option is to install updates automatically. This assumes a broadband link

③ You can specify to download updates in the background, but pick your own time to install them

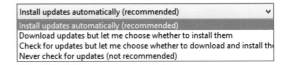

④ Alternatively, you can have Windows Update check for updates and alert you when they are available, but choose for yourself when to both download and install them

Index

U

V

W